Spiders of
Western Canada

SPIDERS
of
WESTERN
CANADA

John Hancock
Kathleen Hancock

LONE
PINE

Lone Pine Publishing
87 Pender Street East
Vancouver, BC
V6A 1S9

Website: www.lonepinepublishing.com

Library and Archives Canada Cataloguing in Publication
Hancock, John, 1935–, author
    Spiders of Western Canada / John W. Hancock and Kathleen M. Hancock.

Includes bibliographical references and index.
ISBN 978-1-55105-916-7 (pbk.)

    1. Spiders—Canada, Western. I. Hancock, Kathleen, 1945–, author II. Title.

QL458.41.C2H36 2015   595.4'409712   C2015-901212-0

Editorial Director: Nancy Foulds
Project Editor: Nicholle Carrière
Editorial: Nicholle Carrière, Sheila Cooke
Production Manager: Leslie Hung
Layout & Production: Gregory Brown
Cover Design: Gerry Dotto, Gregory Brown
Cover photo: jumping spider, itthipolB/Thinkstock
Illustration Credits: all illustrations by John Hancock
Photo Credits: Andre Karwath/Wikipedia, 104; BD/Wikipedia, 167b; Benny Mazur/Flickr, 89b, 91b; Billy Lindblom/Flickr, 70; Buddy H/Thinkstock, 28; D Fletcher/Flickr, 179a; D Sikdes/Flickr, 73; Davefoc/Wikipedia, 167a; David Short/Flickr, 52; Design Pics/Thinkstock, 118; Don Buckle, 47, 65, 111c, 133b, 134, 161; Dudubot/Wikipedia, 71; Fritz Flohr Reynolds/Flickr, 91a; Fyn Kynd/Flickr, 89a; Gail Hampshire/Flickr, 155; gdahlman/Flickr, 86; George Chernilevsky/Wikipedia, 38; Henrik_L/Thinkstock, 24; Jean Shepard, 109b; Kaldari/Flickr, 96; Kathleen Hancock, 9, 26, 27, 32, 37, 41, 82, 109a, 111b, 116, 119, 125, 137b, 144, 165; Knutux/Wikipedia, 36; Lee&Angela Saborio/Wikipedia, 137a; Marshal Hedin/Flickr, 39; Sidersphoto/Thinkstock, 35; Susie3Ford/Thinkstock, 111a; Trappist the Monk/Wikipedia, 132, 133a; USO/Thinkstock 129; Wid Heerbrugg Switzerland, 8

We acknowledge the financial support of the Government of Canada.

Funded by the Government of Canada
Financé par le gouvernement du Canada | Canadä

PC: 30

Contents

Acknowledgements

I was able to make contact with many well-known arachnologists such as Don Buckle, Dr. Robin Leech, Dr. Robert Holmberg and Rick West, who gave help, advice and lists of papers. Don's database of Canadian spiders has been a great help. Dr. Wayne Maddison, Canada Research Chair in Biodiversity and professor at the University of British Columbia, has been a particular help with problem species of Salticidae.

Eight eyes of a spider

It has never ceased to amaze me how willingly this help and advice has been given. With their aid, I began to create a database of the spiders' environment, life history, prey items and how they overwinter. The Shell Waterton Complex, which sponsored me for three years, both financially and through encouragement, offered a great boost.

Six eyes of a spider

Kevin Van Tighem, a biologist working in Waterton Lakes National Park at the time, got me started a few weeks after our arrival in Canada. Cyndi Smith, conservation officer for Waterton Lakes National Park, offered a great deal of help and sponsorship with the database and the illustrated catalogue that I was putting together.

I would like to thank Nicholle Carrière for her patience with my writing, Sheila Quinlan for her work with my first raw draft, and Lone Pine editorial manager Nancy Foulds for making this book possible.

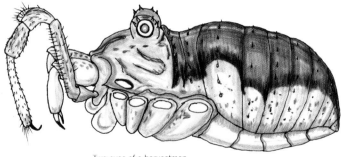

Two eyes of a harvestman

Preface

It is no surprise that the most popular subjects in natural history that appeal to amateur naturalists are birds, flowers and butterflies. But spiders deserve more credit: "In common with most forms of life, spiders are thoroughly fascinating creatures" (Michael J. Roberts, 1995). Michael Roberts is one of my mentors. It was his knowledge of British spiders and his ability to create coloured plates of spiders that stimulated my interest.

Kathleen was born in Whitehead, Northern Ireland, and was educated there. She started her teaching career in London, England. I was born in the City of London, within the sound of the bells of Bow Church, which makes me a true Cockney. World War II interfered with my schooling. It was only when I reached the age of 30 that I really began my education, via the new Open University, while driving a London bus for a living. Therefore, mine is a particular viewpoint—that of an amateur student with a love of the backcountry. I specialize in observations and collecting in the wild. In England, I had some 67 acres to study. Here in western Canada, permits gave me access to over 15 million acres of some of the most beautiful landscape in the world.

Kathleen and I arrived in Canada in 2000 and were made welcome by the people of Pincher Creek, Alberta. We settled down close to Waterton Lakes National Park, and Kevin Van Tighem, the park superintendent, encouraged me to create an inventory of spiders for the park. My first loves have always been true spiders and the outdoors. Can you imagine an amateur with 130,000 acres of wilderness filled with spiders, many of which I had never met before? I loved it, but I wanted to do more than just create a species list; I wanted to study the species. Eventually, my area of study increased to cover the three western provinces of Canada: British Columbia, Alberta and Saskatchewan.

I was turning up a bewildering number of species, and it became necessary to draw every one to make sense of the information I was collecting—hence I became a reluctant artist. Michael Roberts, mentioned above, creates his artwork with coloured inks, while my own attempts are done with coloured pencils.

All the illustrations in this book are mine and are part of a database of some 4000 drawings created via a stereoscopic binocular microscope. Each drawing highlights the spiders' colours beautifully because each fresh specimen is preserved in alcohol, which enhances these colours. With "dry," living specimens, the colours are somewhat duller.

Wild M5 APO binocular
stereomicroscope

In this book, western Canada encompasses British Columbia, Alberta, Saskatchewan and Manitoba. These provinces are very rich in natural regions and include Canadian Shield, boreal forest, aspen parkland, foothills, grasslands, badlands and coastal ecoregions, and feature a variety of climates from subarctic and alpine to hot and arid. The important habitat of spiders is usually a microhabitat that might be found in many ecosystems; for example, a rotten log lying on the ground or the architecture of the branches of a tree, which might be more important to a web-weaving spider rather than the particular species of tree.

In putting this book together, I have tried to illustrate the spiders that you are most likely to come across. Perhaps 50 percent of western Canada's spiders are web weavers, and for this reason, I have featured web-spinning species. Quite often it is the webs that one sees first, and it is a good policy to make a conscious effort to look for them. Don't forget that in life, the web is meant to be invisible, and the observation of webs can be quite an art—you must get the sunlight at the right angle. When just the right conditions are obtained, the web lights up in all its beauty.

As with all observations of wildlife, you need to "stand and stare." It is only when you stop to look that you will see what is around you. Quite often, it is when you stop for lunch and sit down that you will notice webs, a curled leaf or wolf spiders sunning themselves.

There are two other "fun" things that I need to mention. Firstly, spider numbers. I was fortunate to be given a database of spiders that had been recorded in the past. It was compiled by a very talented arachnologist, Don Buckle of Saskatchewan. I have added my own records, and the numbers in this book are from this source, but be warned these numbers are by no way complete.

Secondly, one book and its author that have had a great influence on me is the superb masterpiece *The World of Spiders* (1958), by W.S. Bristowe. He included many illustrations by Arthur Smith, an artist well known for his realistic drawings; my favourite are the spider faces, and for fun and enlightenment, I have included many examples of my own attempts in this book. All my artwork has been created via the microscope shown above.

TARANTULAS • THERAPHOSIDAE	FOLDING-DOOR SPIDERS • ANTRODIAETIDAE	BUZZING OR GHOST SPIDERS • ANYPHAENIDAE

Tarantulas, p. 37	Folding-door Spider, p. 40	Pacific Buzzing Spider, p. 46

SAC SPIDERS • CLUBIONIDAE

Pacific Sac Spider, p. 49	Willow Sac Spider, p. 50	Marsh Sac Spider, p. 51

WOODLOUSE SPIDERS • DYSDERIDAE	STEALTHY GROUND SPIDERS • GNAPHOSIDAE

Woodlouse Spider, p. 53	Common Brown Ground Spider, p. 56	Hooded Gnaphosa, p. 57

STEALTHY GROUND SPIDERS • GNAPHOSIDAE

Day Ground Runner, p. 58	Black Stone Runner, p. 59	Micaria Ant Mimic, p. 60	House Wanderer, p. 61

STEALTHY GROUND SPIDERS • GNAPHOSIDAE | **NARROW-HEADED SPIDERS • LIOCRANIIDAE** | **WOLF SPIDERS • LYCOSIDAE**

Plain Joe Spider, p. 62

Ornate Forest Spider, p. 64

Night Wolf Spider, p. 67

WOLF SPIDERS • LYCOSIDAE

Northern River Wolf Spider, p. 68

Forest Thin-legged Wolf Spider, p. 69

Jesus Spider, p. 70

WOLF SPIDERS • LYCOSIDAE | **PIRATE SPIDERS • MIMETIDAE**

Curtain-door Wolf Spider, p. 72

Turret Spider, p. 74

Cannibal Spider, p. 76

LINK SPIDERS • OXYOPIDAE | **TREE CRAB OR RUNNING CRAB SPIDERS • PHILODROMIDAE**

Lynx Spider, p. 78

Scorpion Crab Spider, p. 81

Grass Crab Spider, p. 82

TREE CRAB OR RUNNING CRAB SPIDERS • PHILODROMIDAE

Cardiac Crab Spider, p. 83   Western Apollo Crab Spider, p. 84   House Running Crab Spider, p. 85

TREE CRAB OR RUNNING CRAB SPIDERS • PHILODROMIDAE   **FISHING OR NURSEY-WEB SPIDERS • PISAURIDAE**

Disparity Crab Spider, p. 86   Variable Running Crab Spider, p. 87   Fishing Spider, p. 90

JUMPING SPIDERS • SALTICIDAE

Zebra Jumping Spider, p. 94   Ant Mimic Jumping Spider, p. 95   Red-backed Jumping Spider, p. 96

JUMPING SPIDERS • SALTICIDAE

Snow Spider, p. 97   Coyote Jumping Spider, p. 98   Hairy Flag Jumping Spider, p. 99

JUMPING SPIDERS • SALTICIDAE

Flag Jumping Spider, p. 100

Feather Flag Jumping Spider, p. 101

Yellow-legs Jumping Spider, p. 102

JUMPING SPIDERS • SALTICIDAE | **SPITTING SPIDERS • SCYTODIDAE** | **VIOLIN OR BROWN SPIDERS • SICARIIDAE**

Peppered Jumper, p. 103

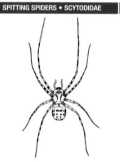

Spitting Spider, p. 105

Violin Spider, p. 107

CRAB SPIDERS • THOMISIDAE

Flower Crab Spider, p. 110

Toad Crab Spider, p. 112

Pirate Crab Spider, p. 113

CRAB SPIDERS • THOMISIDAE

Oviform Crab Spider, p. 114

Triangle Crab Spider, p. 115

Elegant Crab Spider, p. 116

FUNNEL-WEB SPIDERS • AGELENIDAE

Giant House Spider, p. 121   Hobo Spider, p. 122   Grass Funnel-web Spider, p. 123

FUNNEL-WEB SPIDERS • AGELENIDAE   BLUE-SILK SPIDERS • AMAUROBIIDAE

Western Funnel-web Spider, p. 124   Avalanche Spider, p. 127   Hackle-band Spider, p. 128

ORB-WEB WEAVERS • ARANEIDAE

Notch-web Spider, p. 131   Cat Spider, p. 132   Orchard Spider, p. 134

ORB-WEB WEAVERS • ARANEIDAE   MESH-WEB SPIDERS • DICTYNIDAE

Bridge Spider, p. 135   Trashline Spider, p. 136   Western Mesh-ladder Spider, p. 140

MESH-WEB SPIDERS • DICTYNIDAE	SIX-TAILED SPIDERS • HAHNIIDAE	DWARF SHEET-WEB WEAVERS • LINYPHIIDAE

Alberta Mesh-web Spider, p. 141	Six-tailed Spider, p. 143	Cup-and-doily Spider, p. 146

DWARF SHEET-WEB WEAVERS • LINYPHIIDAE

Filmy-dome Spider, p. 147	Spruce Hammock Spider, p. 148	Lasso Money Spider, p. 149

DWARF SHEET-WEB WEAVERS • LINYPHIIDAE

Flying Money Spider, p. 150	Spiny Biceps Spider, p. 151	Pinhead Spider, p. 152

DADDY-LONG-LEGS SPIDERS • PHOLCIDAE	SPOKE-WHEEL SPIDERS • SEGESTRIIDAE

Daddy-long-legs, p. 156	Rock Spider, p. 157	Spoke-wheel Spider, p. 159

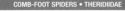

LONG-JAWED OR THICK-JAWED ORBWEAVERS • TETRAGNATHIDAE | **COMB-FOOT SPIDERS • THERIDIIDAE**

Silver Long-jawed Orbweaver, p. 162 | Thick-jawed Hunter, p. 163 | Black Widow, p. 166

COMB-FOOT SPIDERS • THERIDIIDAE

False Widow, p. 168 | House Comb-foot Spider, p. 169 | Fanged Comb-foot Spider, p. 170

COMB-FOOT SPIDERS • THERIDIIDAE

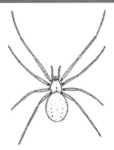

Pale Comb-foot Spider, p. 171 | Ant-eating Comb-foot Spider, p. 172 | Cupboard Spider, p. 173

COMB-FOOT SPIDERS • THERIDIIDAE | **HACKLE-BAND ORBWEAVERS • ULOBORIDAE**

Crusty-head Spider, p. 174 | Triangular-web Spider, p. 177 | Feather-legged Orbweaver, p. 178

INTRODUCTION
Come Face to Face with Spiders

This field guide is designed for the hikers and campers of western Canada. We will describe the fascinating lives of our spiders and describe in detail the common spiders you may meet in your travels and in your garden and home. We will also highlight some spiders that have mind-boggling niches or lifestyles.

This field guide will also be a great help to teachers conducting field trips— there is much advice about the collecting of spiders and their study.

Arachnology is the study of spiders and their kin, whereas arachnophobia is the fear of spiders, from which a number of people suffer, mainly adults. Children are usually quite fascinated by spiders, something we have learned from the many field trips that we have hosted.

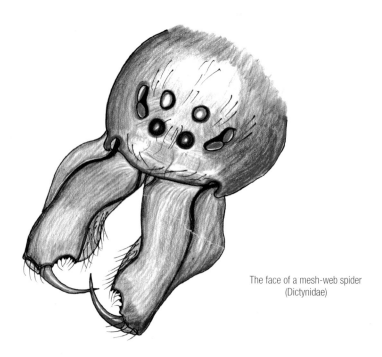

The face of a mesh-web spider
(Dictynidae)

Spiders and Their Kin

Spiders belong to the Class Arachnida in the Order Araneae, which is just one of the 19 orders of the Phylum Chelicerata, which in turn all belong to the Superphylum Arthropoda—creatures with jointed limbs and anterior appendages consisting of a basal segment and a "fang" (see p. 29).

Here are eight of the common orders. There are 11 other minor orders.

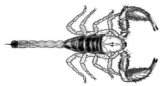

Scorpions
Order Scorpiones
Found in British Columbia, Alberta and Saskatchewan

Spiders
Order Araneae
Very common throughout the world

Pseudoscorpions
Order Pseudoscorpiones
Very small but extremely common

Harvestmen
Order Opiliones
Very common throughout the world

Whip-scorpions
Order Uropygi
Found in the Americas, Africa and Asia

Mites and Ticks
Order Acari
Very common throughout the world

Tailless Whip-scorpions
Order Amblypygi
Found in the Americas, Africa and Asia

Sun Spiders
Order Solifugae
Found in British Columbia, Alberta and Saskatchewan but common throughout the world

Why Spiders?

Many people have a love-hate fascination for spiders, as well as snakes and bats, and these creatures often invoke a mixture of fear, disgust, admiration and wonderment. Sometimes people are indifferent, yet an increasing number are becoming interested in this poorly understood group of creatures. This book is an attempt to open up the world of spiders to the reader, particularly those spiders found in western Canada.

In Canada, we have possibly 1400 different species of spiders divided into some 35 families. Western Canada has 33 families, which contain about 850 species, though the exact number of species remains unknown. Kathleen and I have collected 480 species so far in western Canada, but the number is increasing with each season of work in the field.

It is our hope that this book will draw attention to this important group of invertebrates, their fascinating life cycle and the diversity of niches that they have created in an attempt to parcel out as much of the available food as possible. Herein lies an important message: rich diversity in all forms of life is the key to ensuring the sustainability of life on this planet.

It is our intention to produce detailed drawings of each species of spider to be found in western Canada. With this guide to the families of spiders and some of the more common examples of their genera, we hope to create a lasting interest in the spiders of this region.

Spiders vs. Insects

An insect has six legs, two eyes, a body divided into three parts and antennae in front of the eyes. The adults usually have wings.

Spiders have eight legs, (usually) eight eyes, a body divided into two segments, palps rather than antennae and no wings, though they have found other ways to fly (see p. 33). Consequently, you should not be surprised that spiders are not insects. In fact, they are much older than insects. According to the fossil record, spiders became terrestrial about 250 million years ago; insects began their terrestrial life some 230 million years ago, 20 million years later. I like to think (with poetic licence) that spiders evolved before sex was invented—their reproduction is unlike that of any other terrestrial animal.

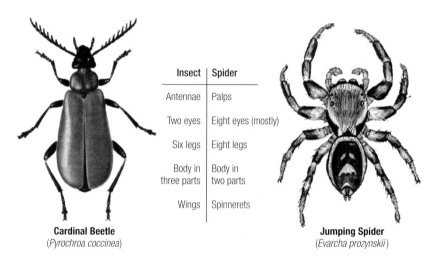

Insect	Spider
Antennae	Palps
Two eyes	Eight eyes (mostly)
Six legs	Eight legs
Body in three parts	Body in two parts
Wings	Spinnerets

Cardinal Beetle
(*Pyrochroa coccinea*)

Jumping Spider
(*Evarcha prozynskii*)

Spiders belong to Arthropoda, the arthropods, which is the largest phylum on Earth. Arthropoda means "jointed foot" and is actually a misnomer—it should really be "jointed leg." All arthropods, including the spiders, have an external skeleton, or exoskeleton, that is typically hard and unyielding to growth. Therefore, to increase in size, the animal must shed (moult) its old skin after creating a new, soft one underneath. The old skin is then discarded. This allows the animal to grow, after which the new exoskeleton hardens. The growth of a spider is, then, a series of moults between birth and mature adult.

The male spider cannot moult once he has reached maturity; he dies within his last skin. The female, if she lives more than one year, can sometimes moult again, becoming a virgin once more when she does so. For more details, see the section on reproduction (p. 22).

Identifying Male and Female Spiders

Adult male and female spiders differ significantly. To demonstrate this, I have chosen to illustrate the Flower Crab Spider, also known as the Goldenrod Crab Spider (*Misumena vatia*), because it shows the differences between the two sexes very well.

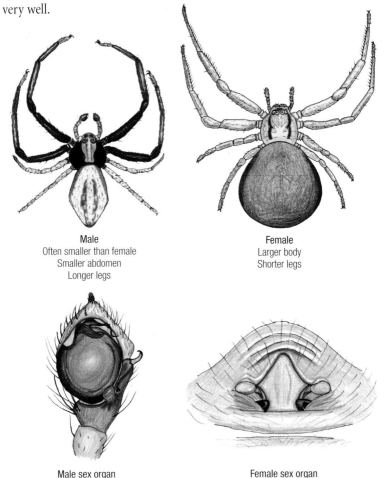

Male
Often smaller than female
Smaller abdomen
Longer legs

Female
Larger body
Shorter legs

Male sex organ
Aperture on underside of anterior abdomen

Female sex organ
Boxing glove–like apparatus on end of palps

Another reason for choosing this species is that the male's palps are not so obviously boxing glove–like. But if you turn the spider over and look at the ventral side of the palps, this structure is easy to see. If in doubt as to whether or not a spider is female, turn it over and view the ventral side, and you will observe the epigynum, the plate that surrounds the sexual aperture.

Spiders and Harvestmen: The Daddy-long-legs Problem

Spiders have bodies that are divided into two visible parts, and they generally have eight eyes, most of them at the front of the head. As a general rule, the web-weaving spiders that you will meet will be hanging upside down from a web.

Harvestmen are members of the Order Opiliones. They are most often seen in autumn, on the outside of your house or garage, often quite high up and in plain sight. Generally, their bodies are not divided (i.e., in a single segment), and they have only two eyes, which are located one-third of the way back on the dorsal side of the head region. They make no web and walk over the substrate the right way up. Although almost all spiders carry poison glands, Harvestmen are not venomous.

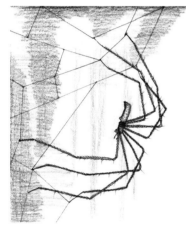

Daddy-long-legs spider

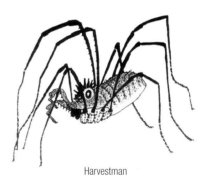

Harvestman

Spider
Body in two sections
Eight eyes

Harvestman (legs excluded)
Body in one fused segment
Two eyes

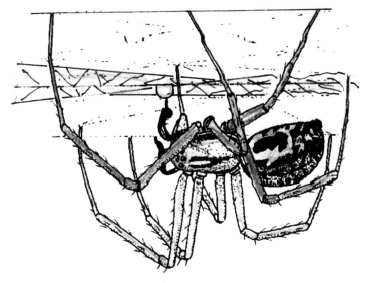

Lephyphantes pollicaris
Male spider on his sperm-web taking up a droplet of sperm

Reproduction

Spider copulation is a very alien affair because the males have no penis. Spiders are a very ancient group of land predators, maybe one of the first to walk on land. Sex, in my opinion, had not been "invented" then. The problem is in the transfer of sperm to the female. Because they lack a penis, the males of most Chelicerates (see p. 17) must produce a drop of sperm, then be able to pick it up and carry it to the female and insert it in some way.

First, the male spider spins a special little web called a sperm web. He then rubs his genital opening across the leading edge of this web, depositing a droplet of sperm. To pick the droplet up, he has a special, modified pair of palps, which look for all the world like shortened legs with boxing gloves on the end. The boxing glove–like organs act like fountain pens—when the male dips a the palp's nib-like structure into the droplet of sperm, the fluid is sucked up into a reservoir-like bulb.

The males of Theraphosidae, the tarantulas, have very simple palps (see p. 37). True spiders have much more complex palpal structures.

Illustrated below are the last two segments of an immature palp and a male palp as it would look after the spider's last moult, when it has reached maturity. When the male spider's palps are primed for mating, he goes in search of a female.

Immature or female palp

Mature male palp

Courtship

A male spider's courtship can be dangerous. He can be stabbed by the female's fangs and venom inserted, he may be injured in some way or he may even be eaten. Spiders are carnivorous, and males and females live separate lives until mating time. To mate, the male must persuade the female that he is not a meal, but a healthy male come a-courting. He does this by performing a courtship display. Once the male has pacified the female, he will insert the "nib" of his palp into the female and squeeze out sperm into a special pouch in the female's abdomen called a spermatheca, where it is stored. The sperm remains in the spermatheca until egg-laying time, when it is mixed with the eggs, fertilizing them and creating the next generation of spiders.

Courting male jumping spider

The female spins a cocoon of silk in which she lays her eggs. The silk cocoon protects the eggs from the elements and predators, and quite often, the eggs or spiderlings survive winter in this way.

The spiderlings hatch and then develop through a series of moults. All arthropods moult. Spiders, in common with most invertebrates, have a rigid exoskeleton that restricts growth. So, to grow, a spider must shed its entire "skin." Everything that is on or part of the exoskeleton is shed—all the hairs, spinnerets, claws and lenses of the eyes—and internal organs are shed as well, including the book lungs and trachea, as well as the spermatheca and, believe it or not, the sucking stomach.

Techniques for Observing Spiders

There is a great deal of information available about the identification of spiders, but very little about the daily life of spiders. So here, I am going to dwell on the various ways of observing spiders.

While on a walk or hike, a good hiker will keep his or her eyes on the ground. It is there that you will see your first wolf spiders. Take a closer look. Some will be actively hunting and move quite fast, whereas others will be towing an egg sac attached to their spinnerets. Some females will appear "fuzzy" owing to a mass of spiderlings hitching a ride on their mother's back; the female will carry them until they are ready to moult.

Wolf spider with babies

As I have often said, the student needs only to stand and stare. Quite often when on a walk or hike, it is only when you stop for lunch that you have time to observe. Perhaps the best method to observe spiders while sitting is to use a pair of low-power binoculars. I find an 8X10 magnification comfortable to use, and these binoculars will focus down to about 3 metres, giving you a wonderful close-up view of spiders. It is also possible to fit a pair of close-up lenses for higher magnifications. You will be surprised at how exciting these close-up views are; tiny items that you would not have noticed before will entertain you for some time.

Orb web of *Argiope trifasciata* with stabilimentum

Another method you should try is to just carefully examine the leaves, looking for unnatural curled shapes. Once you have "got your eye in," as we arachnologists like to say, spotting what you're looking for becomes easy. This is an important concept to understand, so bear with me. If you are searching for spiders under rocks, for example, you want to have a mental picture of what you are looking for before you start. You will be surprised at what you will miss without having "got your eye in" as a mental picture.

Getting back to the curled leaves, you will also learn to spot the give-away threads of silk around a curled leaf, most often a green one. Many species of spiders use green leaves as a retreat. Often you may see a ticklish silken thread stretching out from this retreat. It is the bridging line of an orb-web spider. The familiar sticky spiral catching web will have been taken down, leaving only the bridging line visible. If you know what to look for, you can surprise your friends with your wonderful eyesight.

While on the move, watch for spider webs. Most webs are hard to see because the silk is very fine. In fact, they are meant not to be seen, so you must get the sun in a favourable position to be able to see them at all. Some orb webs are made conspicuous by a bright silver band, called a stabilimentum, either across the diameter or as a circle at the web's hub. One species, the Trashline Spider (*Cyclosa conica*), creates a vertical line of debris and "bones" from her last meal (see p. 136). Check the ground for sheet webs and funnel webs. On dry, dusty days or beside dusty gravel roads, these ground-hugging webs can easily be seen.

Collecting pot

Collecting Spiders

One of the simplest methods of collecting spiders is to use a small container (collecting pot) such as one that prescription medications come in, and simply encourage the spider to walk in. A good size for the container is 3x8 centimetres. This depth and width prevents the spider from running out once it has been caught.

You may wish to make a "pooter" to catch smaller spiders. A pooter is simply three pieces of plastic tube, where the middle piece has a smaller bore than the other two. The middle section fits into and joins all three pieces to form one length, making a pooter. If you place one end close to a given spider, then suck in at the other end, the spider is drawn into the tube. I hasten to add that a cloth filter is essential to prevent the spider from entering your mouth.

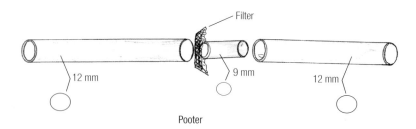

Filter

12 mm   9 mm   12 mm

Pooter

A good method of collecting spiders from various types of vegetation is to use a sweep net. I have seen such nets for sale that our local UFA (United Farmers of Alberta) store. Spider researchers divide the environment into a number of layers or levels related to the spiders' preferred niche—the ground, field, shrub and tree layers.

Sweep net

To sample the field layer, you simply walk, swinging the net from side to side. To collect from shrubs and trees, simply hold the net under the foliage and beat the branches with your hiking stick. Use your pooter to extract the spiders of interest and return the rest to their source.

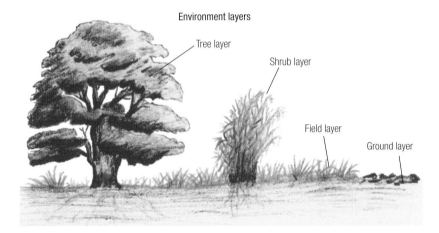
Environment layers
Tree layer
Shrub layer
Field layer
Ground layer

Studying Spiders by Habitat

On the whole, each spider species is found in a particular microhabitat, and this is quite often only loosely related to the surrounding environment. Yet some spiders do have a preference for a particular kind of habitat. For example, we have a number of non-native spiders that have been introduced from warmer climates, and these are quite often found within our homes or outbuildings.

Orb-web spiders are not usually found on any particular species of plant. What is important to an orb-web weaver is the architecture of the branches of the plant, shrub or tree—they need to be fairly rigid. Good trees to sample are the spruces, owing to the dense clumps of needles that offer protection and good anchorage for various web designs.

Quite a few species of jumping spiders prefer hot, rocky outcrops where flies like to land and sun themselves. Jumping spiders are daylight hunters that stalk their prey with the aid of very keen eyesight. Likewise, wolf spiders are hunters of the ground zone, stalking their prey by sight, and can often be readily seen on hot, sunny days. A few species of different families are associated with ants, which they mimic in surprising detail. Many species of ground spiders are most easily found under rocks, whereas blue-silk spiders can be found under bark or inside rotting logs. Most crab spiders are ambush predators, and some specialize in preying on pollinating insects. By sitting in a flower, very still and camouflaged to some extent, they obtain an easy living and may be the laziest spiders in the world.

Hammock web among pine needles

Spider Anatomy

Few people may be interested in the anatomy of spiders, but to follow the journey through this book, a little understanding is necessary.

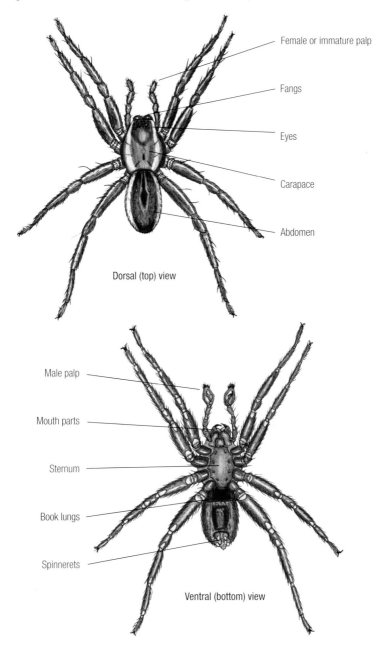

Female or immature palp

Fangs

Eyes

Carapace

Abdomen

Dorsal (top) view

Male palp

Mouth parts

Sternum

Book lungs

Spinnerets

Ventral (bottom) view

Appendages

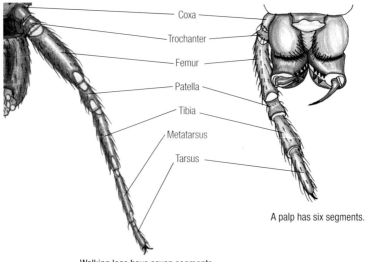

Coxa
Trochanter
Femur
Patella
Tibia
Metatarsus
Tarsus

A palp has six segments.

Walking legs have seven segments.

The metatarsus and the tarsus of the walking legs are really an extension of the tarsus, so the metatarsus is technically a false segment.

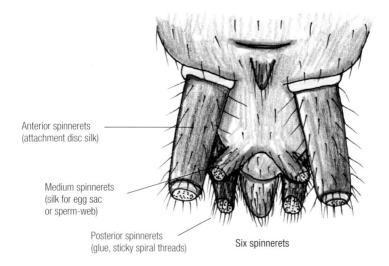

Anterior spinnerets
(attachment disc silk)

Medium spinnerets
(silk for egg sac
or sperm-web)

Posterior spinnerets
(glue, sticky spiral threads)

Six spinnerets

The spinnerets produce the spider's silk. There are three pairs of spinnerets, and each pair has a different function and produces a different kind of silk.

Chelicerae

The paired chelicerae are the first appendages on the spider's "head." They carry the fangs along with the poison glands.

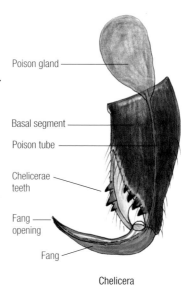

Chemically, spider venom contains many different substances. The venom of a Black Widow, for example, has seven different proteins. The effects of a Black Widow's bite include rapid heartbeat, increased blood pressure, breathing difficulties and paralysis. Death can occur in rare cases.

All spider families have poison glands except one, the hackle-band orbweavers (Uloboridae). All spiders except members of this family are potentially venomous to their prey. Only about 30 species out of some 38,000 are dangerous to humans.

Poison gland

Basal segment

Poison tube

Chelicerae teeth

Fang opening

Fang

Chelicera

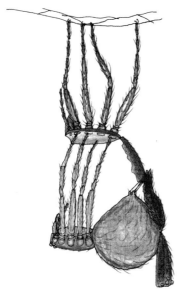

Moulting spider

The Moult

The rigid exoskeleton of spiders, as well as all other arthropods, restricts growth because the head region and appendages cannot expand within it. Therefore, growth can occur only when the spider moults. During the moulting process, a new "skin" develops underneath the old, and when the time is right, the spider hangs upside down from its web or from silken strands (in the case of web-weaving spiders; hunting spiders, on the other hand, moult within a silk retreat). In the case of a web-weaving spider, the exoskeleton covering the spider's head splits in two across the "forehead." Next, the split travels right around the head region, and then around the body, stopping at the spinnerets.

Cast exoskeleton of a tarantula. In shedding its skin, the tarantula also sheds its eye lenses.

The spider now falls out of its old exoskeleton, aided by gravity and prevented from falling any farther by silk threads anchored to the old skin. It takes some hours for the new skin to harden, and the spider cannot feed until this happens. It should be noted that males form complex palps at maturity and cannot successfully rebuild a new exoskeleton, so they die in their last mature moult.

The photograph above shows the cast exoskeleton of a tarantula from Mexico. The spider herself is probably still alive; some females live for 25 years, yet a male's lifespan is only a few years. In Canada, most spiders are annual, living for just one year; the species survive the winter as eggs. Some spiders live for two years and others live for a few years.

In shedding her "skin," the female tarantula also sheds her eye lenses, as well as the entire outer covering of her legs, palps, spinnerets and fangs. It may be hard to believe, but she also sheds her sucking stomach, book lungs and spermathecae. The spermathecae is where she stores any received sperm. If she does not want the sperm, she can moult instead.

Every time a female spider moults after maturity, she becomes a virgin again. Note that most "true spiders" die after their maturity, moult. We can learn a lot from studying tarantulas owing to their long life and large size, which makes observation easier.

Feeding

Spiders can only take in liquid food. A spider, on catching a prey item, will first bite it on an extremity, such as a leg. This way, the spider avoids injury when tackling a struggling insect. When it bites, a spider inflicts two holes in the prey's leg; it has two fangs that close like a pair of scissors. After biting its prey, the spider injects venom, which quickly paralyzes the victim. Through the two tiny holes it has made, the spider pumps in powerful digestive juices that break down the victim's flesh into a "soup." Then, and only then, can the spider suck out the contents of the insect prey.

If you find dead flies on your window ledge, and if they are remains of a spider's meal, they will be just empty shells. The special sucking stomach of a spider can both eject fluid and suck fluid up into the digestive tract. This liquefied food is sucked through the spider's narrow mouth, which prevents large particles from passing into the digestive system. A second filtration occurs in the pharynx, which is lined with thousands of "platelets" arranged like shingles; only very small particles can pass through this filter.

The females of some spider species can feed their young ones via mouth-to-mouth action. The young are fed a special substance that the female spider regurgitates.

How Spiders Fly

Spiders have no wings, yet they can span great distances. Have you ever wondered how a spider spins a web across a gap of several metres? It floats a line of silk out on a breeze. The silk is very light, stronger than steel and produced at will. Once the floating line has attached itself to an object, the spider can span the void by using its eight legs and tightroping, suspended underneath the silken thread. Also, once this thread, or bridging line, is created, the web can be built.

Flying (also called ballooning) is a similar process. The spider climbs to a high point and sticks its behind up into the air. It then squirts silk into the breeze, which carries the line away until it is many metres in length. This length will now support the weight of the spider, and at this point, the spider lets go of its perch. Each year, millions of spiders migrate from fields to forests by ballooning.

While ballooning, the spider can regulate its flight to some extent by shortening or lengthening the flight line. In fact, special aircraft sampling the atmosphere, have collected spiders at altitudes as high as 3 kilometres.

About This Book

In organizing this field guide, first we have drawn attention to the hunting spiders that you will see running on the ground as you walk, followed by the web-weaving spiders, whose webs you will probably see first. We will also highlight some species that have specialized niches or lifestyles.

The interested public, we believe, prefers to have common names for the spiders that they observe. Yet this is a problem area because there is often more than one common name for a species, and these names can be quite misleading. We have carefully chosen common names that describe each spider, and most conform to the American Arachnology common names list. Common names really need to be standardized; for example, a beautiful crab spider that is typically seen sitting in flowers has the common name of Goldenrod Crab Spider. The problem is that goldenrod plants flower very late in the year, and this spider, immature or adult, will settle on whatever flowers happen to be blooming at the time. These spiders adopt a variety flowering plant as "feeding platforms" and are found on plants other than goldenrods. With this in mind, we prefer to call this species Flower Crab Spider.

All species have a scientific name that is more precise than a common name. In the case of the Flower Crab Spider, the scientific name is *Misumena vatia* (Clerck, 1757), and this is the name used by arachnologists all over the world. The first part of the scientific name, which is always capitalized and italicized, is the genus that the spider belongs to. The second part of the name, which is always lowercase and italicized, is its species name. The name of the author who first described the species, also called the authority, and the year of the publication of a paper follows; if the author's name is in brackets, it means that the name of the genus has been changed, but the name of the authority and date remain the same.

Note that for each species, the size and descriptions refer to the female. The males are typically smaller and more inconspicuous—the spiders that you see will most often be female.

Regarding the spider numbers used in the book—I was fortunate to be given a database of spiders that had been compiled by a very talented arachnologist, Don Buckle of Saskatchewan. I have added my own records, and the numbers in this book are from this source, but be warned that they are in no way complete. All data given regarding species numbers and other statistics is accurate to the year 2010.

HUNTING
SPIDERS

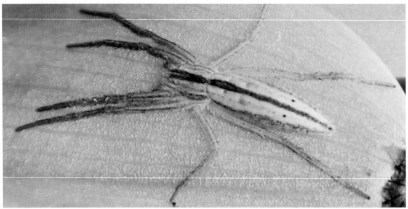
Grass Crab Spider (*Tibellus oblongus*)

HUNTING SPIDERS

We will deal first with spiders that use various hunting strategies rather than building webs because hunting may have been primitive spiders' way of obtaining food. Also, it allows us to start with the infraorder Mygalomorphae, which is more "primitive," or closer to the ancestors of "true spiders." Yet bear in mind that all spiders produce silk, even hunting spiders that do not create a snare in the form of a catching web of silk. Silk is used for many purposes, including to build a retreat, line a burrow or spin a dragline.

Most hunting spiders have just two claws at the end of each leg, yet there are exceptions. For example, the Wolf Spider's ancestors were web-spinning spiders that reverted to hunting. Many hunting spiders are diurnal, or daytime hunters, though an equal number are active at night, being nocturnal hunters. A good sample of both night and day hunters can obtained with the aid of a pitfall trap because most of these spiders are ground hunters. Using a flashlight is a great help in finding nocturnal species because many have "reflectors" behind their eyes that that make the eyes shine back at you.

Hunting strategies take a number of forms. For example, the jumping spiders (Salticidae) use a stalk-and-pounce type of hunting. This requires good eyesight, which goes along with having large eyes.

Other species, such as the crab spiders, are ambush predators that lie in wait for their prey. These spiders often have very cryptic coloration that camouflages them in their surroundings. Still other species lie in wait within a burrow or retreat and may use trip wires as a warning device.

Tarantulas and Their Kin
Infraorder Mygalomorphae

Although no tarantula (Theraphosidae) species are found in Canada, four genera of mygalomorphs have been recorded here, containing five species. Western Canada has four species recorded so far, but no tarantulas (Theraphosidae). They have been included here because they are popular pets and provide a useful way of studying spiders.

Tarantulas, also known as mygalomorphs, are very different from the true spiders that we meet in everyday life. Only five species have been found in Canada, as far as I know, and four of these are from British Columbia.

Chilean Rose Tarantula (*Grammostola spatulata*), the ideal pet species for a beginner.

Mexican Red-knee *(Euathlus smithi)*, female.
This tropical species is sold to the pet trade and is not found in western Canada.

The male tarantula cannot moult once he has reached maturity; he will die within his last skin. The female, if she lives for more than one year, can moult again, and in doing so, she becomes a virgin again. For more details, see the section on reproduction (p. 22).

Simple mature palp

To identify a mygalomorph, look for these three features:

Fangs that strike downward

Four book-lungs

Eyes grouped together on a turret

Spiders in this family are named for the four types of burrow entrances that they create: trapdoor spiders, turret spiders, curtain-door spiders and folding-door spiders. All of them excavate a burrow and cover the entrance with a door of some sort, making it difficult to find the burrow. At night, the door is left open, and the spider strikes at any passing prey.

Folding-door Spiders
Antrodiaetidae

Spiders in this family are named for the four types of burrow entrances that they create: trapdoor spiders, turret spiders, curtain-door spiders and folding-door spiders. All of them excavate a burrow and cover the entrance with a door of some sort, making it difficult to find the burrow. At night, the door is left open, and the spider strikes at any passing prey.

Antrodiaetus unicolor, female. This species is not found in western Canada.

FOLDING-DOOR SPIDER

Antrodiaetus pacificus (Simon, 1884)

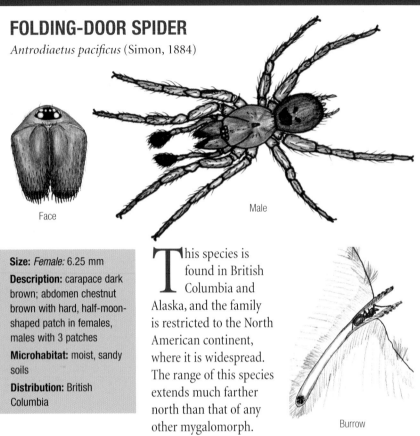

Face

Male

Burrow

Size: *Female:* 6.25 mm
Description: carapace dark brown; abdomen chestnut brown with hard, half-moon-shaped patch in females, males with 3 patches
Microhabitat: moist, sandy soils
Distribution: British Columbia

This species is found in British Columbia and Alaska, and the family is restricted to the North American continent, where it is widespread. The range of this species extends much farther north than that of any other mygalomorph. It is mainly found along the Pacific coast in humid, cool, rather densely forested habitats with deep loam or sandy soil.

This spider's burrow is slightly wider at the entrance than at the bottom. Also, the silk lining of the burrow is thickest at the upper end. The entrance has a flexible silken collar with particles of soil embedded; it is kept collapsed during the day and is very hard to find. At night, look for it with the aid of a flashlight. The spider waits just inside the entrance to strike at any passing prey that approaches too close. Quite often, you can see the spider's eyes shining in the light.

The male, once he reaches maturity, leaves his burrow, never to return, and goes in search of a female in her burrow. Shortly after mating, the male dies; he is unable to moult once his palps metamorphose into the elaborate sexual organs of a mature spider.

The female is quite long-lived. Each year she moults, casting off her old skin along with her stomach lining and spermathecae, making her a virgin every year.

True Spiders
Infraorder Araneomorphae

Flower Crab Spider (*Misumena vatia*), an ambush predator.

True spiders, or araneomorphs, number over 38,000 species worldwide. North America has about 3600 species, and Canada has about 1400 species recorded so far. Western Canada has something like 1000 species. True spiders are our most common spiders—there are few mygalomorphs west of the Rockies.

Identifying true spiders requires a different, more exacting study than recognizing mygalomorphs. For simplication, we have grouped the true spiders into two feeding strategies: hunting, which possibly came first, and web weaving, or constructing a snare.

True spiders have fangs that operate in a pincher-like fashion. Their eyes are usually widely separated, and their spinnerets have just two segments. If the spider you are looking at has these characteristics, most likely it is a true spider. Some of the other characteristics to look for are a single pair of book-lungs and eight or fewer eyes.

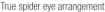
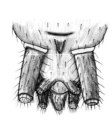

True spider eye arrangement   True spider spinnerets

Book-lungs

For identification purposes, true spiders can be divided into three groups:
- cribellate spiders
- haplogyne spiders
- entelegyne spiders

Cribellate Spiders

Most of the species in this category have a cribellum plate and a comb-like row of hairs called the calamistrum. With this apparatus, these spiders produce a non-sticky silk that is designed to entangle the legs of their prey with combed-out, or hackled, silk.

It is now thought that all cribellate spiders and all orb-web weavers evolved as one, and that the cribellum and its calamistrum were primitive features of all true spiders that have been lost in a large number of species.

Cribellum plate

Haplogyne Spiders

Most of these spiders have six eyes and a primitive form of genitalia in which the female lacks a sclerotized (hardened) epigynum.

Six eyes

Entelegyne Spiders

This group includes the vast majority of living spiders. Most of these spiders have eight eyes. The female has external copulatory openings set on a sclerotized epigynum. The fangs operate with a side-to-side action.

The wolf spider is a hunter.

Probably the first type of true spider you will think of is the orb-web spider. The orb web is a unique method of catching prey. Very few animals snare their prey this way—it is the spider's niche, or its profession.

Eight eyes and fangs with side-to-side action

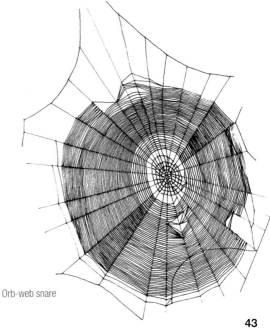

Orb-web snare

43

Buzzing or Ghost Spiders
Anyphaenidae

Face

Four genera of Anyphaenidae have been recorded in Canada, containing seven species. Our region of Canada has two species recorded so far from British Columbia, Alberta and Saskatchewan.

The spiders of this family are long-legged hunters that live mainly in trees and shrubs. Some can be found hunting over the leaf litter on the forest floor. They make no web to trap their prey, but stalk and then pounce, sinking their fangs into their victim and injecting venom, which quickly subdues the "meal."

A male drumming on conifer needles with his palps and vibrating the air with his front pair of legs (redrawn after Bristowe, 1958)

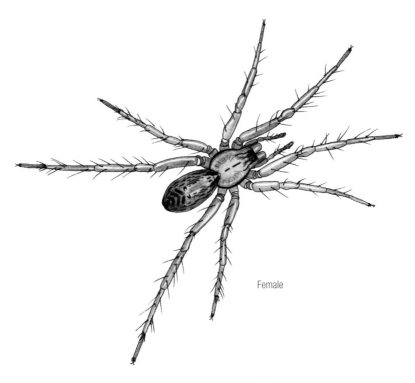

Female

Prey is often detected by a sense we may find hard to understand, that of "touch at a distance." This sense is the product of extremely long, fine hairs that sit in special sockets. In some spider species, these hairs are arranged in rows of various heights toward the tips of the legs. The slightest air current, such as that caused by an insect's wings or a sound, makes these hairs quiver.

Buzzing spiders get their common name from the courtship of the male, which uses a leaf as a sounding board. The male will approach a female while walking with jerky steps and vibrating his abdomen by tapping it violently against the substrate, making a sound that is clearly audible. It is a bit like the buzzing of a fly. One wonders if this behaviour arose among spiders living in broadleaf trees, as this medium would act as a more efficient sounding board, though the species in this area are most frequently found among conifers.

I have collected mature males as early as March. The female lays her eggs in late June through to July. The egg sac is either attached to the underside of a leaf, and the leaf edge is curled over or inserted between the scales of a pine cone. The female stands guard over the egg sac until she dies, usually in autumn.

PACIFIC BUZZING SPIDER

Anyphaena pacifica (Banks, 1896)
Anyphaena aperta (Banks, 1921)

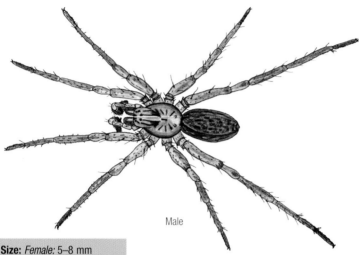

Male

Size: *Female:* 5–8 mm

Description: carapace orange with dark margins; abdomen pale orange with 4–5 chevrons

Microhabitat: tree foliage

Distribution: British Columbia, Alberta and Saskatchewan

Ventral view of abdomen showing tracheal spiracle in the middle
(*A. aperta*)

This species is mainly tree dwelling, particularly in conifers (spruces) near water, and is found throughout western Canada. It is a nocturnal hunter.

There are some seven species of this family that occur in Canada (Platnick, 1974). *A. pacifica* is the one most likely to be found in western Canada. Some species overwinter as subadults under rocks and among leaf litter. This may give them an early start in the spring by allowing them to mate early and produce two generations per year.

The female has little use of silk as a snare but uses it for the construction of a sac-like retreat, which is rebuilt every few days. Also, she creates a beautiful silk egg sac, which is often wrapped up in a leaf or placed among the scales of a pine cone.

One easy way to identify this species is to turn it over and observe the conspicuous tracheal spiracle uniquely placed in the centre of the abdomen.

Sac Spiders
Clubionidae

Three genera of Clubionidae have been recorded across Canada, containing 35 species. Our region has 21 species.

Sac spiders get their name from the silken retreats they make within folded leaves. They are mainly nocturnal hunters and spend the daytime in their silken sacs among vegetation, under stones or underneath the bark of trees.

The sac is a retreat, often containing a female, her egg sac or spiderlings

These spiders have a special pad of hairs on the tips of their "feet" and claw tufts. The end of each hair is split into thousands of finer extensions called end feet. Each hair has between 500 and 1000 end feet. Experts are unsure how the spider is capable of walking upside down on a surface. It is not known just how the end feet work.

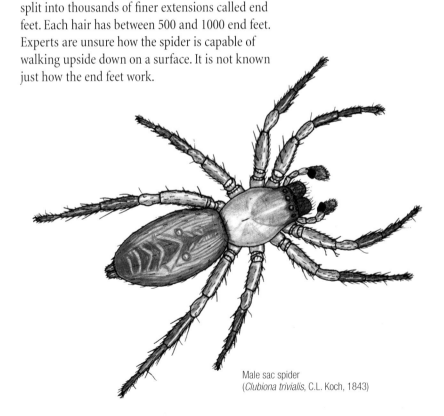

Male sac spider
(*Clubiona trivialis*, C.L. Koch, 1843)

47

Typical sac spider
(*Clubiona canadensis*, Banks, 1890)

Sac spider face

The carapace of sac spiders is typically yellow-orange or plain yellow-brown, and the abdomen is often a dull brownish or reddish grey with a "mousy" look, or pubescence. In some species, there is a distinct mark at the midline and at the front of the abdomen. This is the cardiac mark, which outlines the spider's heart. Although spiders have an open blood system (the blood is contained within sinuses rather than vessels, unlike our own circulatory system), a heart is still required to circulate the blood. Among the many families of spiders, one can often see the cardiac mark, which sometimes creates a visually pleasing pattern.

PACIFIC SAC SPIDER

Clubiona pacifica (Banks, 1896)

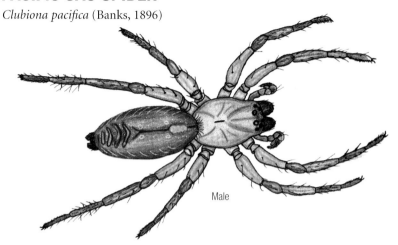

Male

This spider, as its name implies, is a Pacific Coast species that is found mainly in British Columbia and also in southwestern Alberta. Its main habitat is the field layer among grasses and shrubs, along salt marshes and lakeshores and in subalpine meadows. It can often be identified by viewing the female epigynum or the male palp with a 20x hand lens.

Size: *Female:* 6–7 mm
Description: carapace yellow-orange; abdomen dull red
Microhabitat: field layer
Distribution: British Columbia and Alberta

Members of this family do not spin webs to catch prey, but hunt at night by stealth; they have only two claws on each leg (web-spinning spiders have three claws per leg, which enables them to move across their webs without falling; most live out their lives on the underside of a web). The pair of claws is often surrounded by special hairs called scopulae, which enable the spider to walk upside down, for example, on the underside of a leaf. A very similar species, *C. canadensis*, is common in the parkland and boreal forest regions of Alberta, Saskatchewan and Manitoba.

Female epigynum

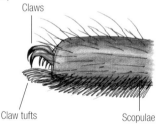

Claws

Claw tufts

Scopulae

Two-clawed hunter's tarsus

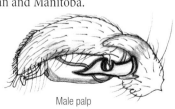

Male palp

WILLOW SAC SPIDER

Clubiona lutescens (Westring, 1851)

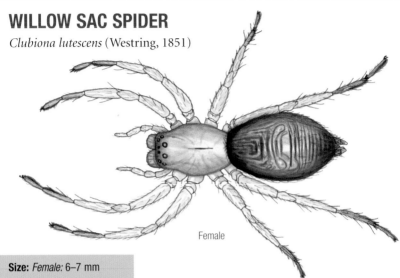

Female

Size: *Female:* 6–7 mm

Description: carapace yellow-orange; abdomen dull red

Microhabitat: moist grasses and shrubs

Distribution: British Columbia; introduced from Europe

Male palp dorsal view

Male palp ectal view

This species of wetlands and moist forests is most commonly found on shrubs bordering marshy areas. It prefers humid places among grasses and low shrubs. The best way to observe this spider is to look for rolled-up leaves. Gently pick the leaf and unroll it into a container. You will most likely find a female with an egg sac or a tangled mass of spiderlings.

The male, on finding a female's retreat in a curled leaf, will drum on the leaf to let her know of his presence. Then he will tear a hole in the silk holding the leaf together, roughly grasp her in his jaws and proceed to mate with her. The male has a very slender body that likely helps him quickly enter the female's retreat.

On the right is a curled leaf retreat of the Willow Sac Spider. Note that the leaf is curled under. This has an advantage to the female spider and her eggs or spiderlings

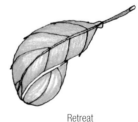

Retreat

because the stomata or breathing pores on the underside of the leaf maintain the desired humidity.

MARSH SAC SPIDER

Clubiona riparia (L. Koch, 1866)

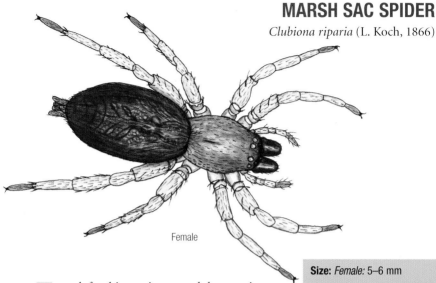

Female

Look for this species around the margins of beaver ponds, ponds with still water and shallow lakes. It is found right across western Canada.

The best way to observe spiders is to stop, stand still and look around you. For sac spiders, which are nocturnal hunters, look for their retreats, and in this species, for a blade of grass or sedge with its top folded over. If you see this, take a close look; the spider will have folded the tip of a sedge leaf blade back on itself and then forward again, creating a beautiful, three-sided box. The whole is held together by the silken sac within. As outlined in the previous species account, the stomata, or breathing pores, on the underside of the leaf maintain the desired humidity for the female spider and her eggs or spiderlings. The Marsh Sac Spider is capable of climbing vertical substrates such as grasses and sedges, and you will often find its retreat on a downward-folded sedge leaf.

Size: *Female:* 5–6 mm

Description: carapace yellow to dark orange; abdomen red-brown

Microhabitat: marsh grasses

Distribution: British Columbia, Alberta, Saskatchewan and Manitoba

Sac retreat

Face

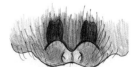

Female epigynum

Woodlouse Spiders
Dysderidae

Dysderids are nocturnal ground hunters. These European spiders were introduced into this country, along with their prey, the woodlouse or sowbug.

Six-eyed hunter

This family has only a single genus, which contains just one species in Canada. It has only recently been found in western Canada.

Woodlouse Spider (*Dysdera crocata*)

WOODLOUSE SPIDER

Dysdera crocata (C.L. Koch, 1838)

Female

Size: *Female:* 11–15 mm

Description: carapace plain red; abdomen orange-brown

Microhabitat: on the ground under rocks and among heaps of old horse manure

Distribution: British Columbia; introduced from Europe

This unusual six-eyed spider (it has lost the anterior medium eyes) is an immigrant from Europe. It builds no web, for it is a nocturnal, wandering hunter. The common name refers to its main prey, terrestrial isopods such as woodlice, also known as sowbugs, which are also introduced species. Its particularly long fangs help it deal with this type of prey.

In western Canada, the Woodlouse Spider is found only in southern coastal British Columbia and occurs mostly in urban areas and disturbed habitats.

The best way to find this spider is by raking through old, dry horse manure heaps, which typically have a huge community of prey items. These decaying heaps of compost are a haven for detritovores such as woodlice. They chew dead plant material into small fragments and deposit these as fecal pellets, which decompose rapidly. This spider is the only known animal that preys exclusively on woodlice.

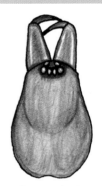

Carapace, showing eye arrangement

Woodlouse or sowbug

53

Stealthy Ground Spiders
Gnaphosidae

Fifteen genera have been recorded in Canada, containing 88 species. Western Canada has 71 species recorded so far in 15 genera. This high number of species can probably be attributed to the rocky nature of the western areas of Canada.

Members of the family Gnaphosidae are noctural ground hunters. This group of spiders is possibly most abundant in our drier and more mountainous areas. It lives and hunts under stones or plant debris. Most members of this family are nocturnal hunters, do not construct a snare (web of silk) and are greyish brown

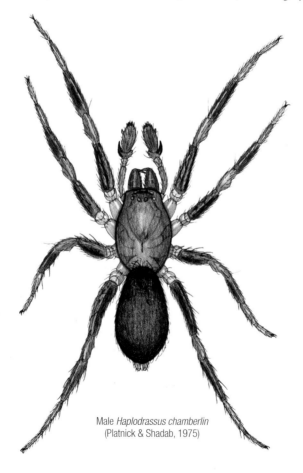

Male *Haplodrassus chamberlin*
(Platnick & Shadab, 1975)

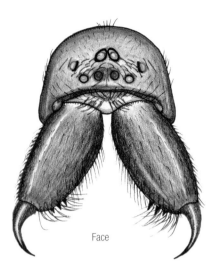

Face

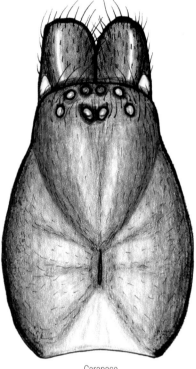

Carapace

to jet black. Some members of the Gnaphosidae family have enlarged chelicerae and fangs. The females are good mothers, building an extensive silken cell in which to lay their eggs, where they guard them until the spiderlings disperse. Then the female dies, her life complete.

The genus *Zelotes* is group of nocturnal black ground spiders in this family. These spiders are handsome but not often seen unless you look for them—it may be necessary to turn over rocks to observe them. In fact, you are more likely to see their egg sacs than the spiders themselves. These egg sacs are shaped like poached eggs and are stuck to the undersides of rocks. The egg sacs have an outer flange that looks like an egg white and a domed centre that resembles a yolk (see p. 59). In reality, the domed area houses the spider's eggs. The whole is a beautiful pink and has the texture of parchment. These egg sacs can be found during every month of the year, though they will often be empty, the spiderlings having dispersed. An egg sac may last a couple of years.

COMMON BROWN GROUND SPIDER

Haplodrassus signifer (C.L. Koch, 1839)

Male

Size: *Female:* 7.5–9 mm

Description: carapace orange with dark eye region; abdomen dark brown with central beige patch

Microhabitat: on the ground under rocks and in damp habitats

Distribution: British Columbia, Alberta and Saskatchewan

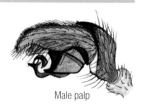

Male palp

Female epigynum

The Common Brown Ground Spider is a stealth hunter and, being nocturnal, spends the daylight hours hidden in a silken retreat. To meet this species, you must look for it, and the easiest way to do so is to turn over slab rocks, where you will find its retreat and the spider within.

As its common name implies, this is a very common spider, and I have found it particularly among rocky landscapes in high alpine regions. It also occurs in a multitude of other habitats. The Common Brown Ground Spider has been reported from prairie grasslands and wheat fields right down to sea level among salt marshes. It is also found under and within rotten logs in grasslands and coniferous forests.

The spinnerets of most ground spiders are cylindrical.

This spider ranges over a very large area of North America, south to Mexico and north to Yukon Territory and Greenland. In fact, its range extends right across northern Europe and Asia.

HOODED GNAPHOSA

Gnaphosa muscorum (C.L. Koch, 1866)

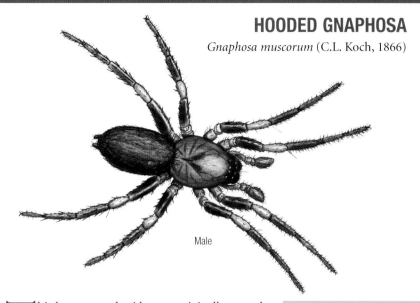

Male

This large ground spider was originally named *Gnaphosa gigantea*. Its common name refers to the female's epigynum, which has a large hood above the median septum; this can be seen with the aid of a 10X hand lens. The male's palps are also conspicuous in this species.

This spider is common right across western Canada. It is typically found among rocks and stones, particularly in spruce and pine forests. It has also been reported on sandy soils and in grasslands. The Hooded Gnaphosa is considered to be strictly Holarctic, occurring mainly in alpine and subarctic habitats to elevations as high as 4500 metres.

This species, like most ground spiders, is a nocturnal hunter that remains within a silken retreat during the day. The male in particular is a great wanderer. The mature female may be found guarding a characteristically flattened egg sac, which can contain up to 250 eggs.

There are about 25 *Gnaphosa* species recorded in North America, and 12 of these are found in Canada and Alaska (Platnick and Shadab, 1975a).

Size: *Female:* 10–12 mm
Description: carapace plain orange; abdomen plain brown
Microhabitat: on the ground under rocks
Distribution: British Columbia, Alberta, Saskatchewan and Manitoba

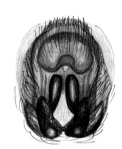

Female's "hooded" epigynum

Male palp

57

DAY GROUND RUNNER

Gnaphosa parvula (Banks, 1896)

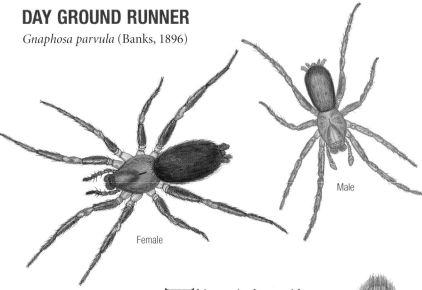

Male

Female

Size: *Female:* 8–10 mm

Description: carapace light brown; abdomen dark grey

Microhabitat: on the ground under rocks

Distribution: British Columbia, Alberta, Saskatchewan and Manitoba

This species has a wide range from Alaska right down to Colorado, east to Newfoundland and south to West Virginia. However, most *Gnaphosa* species are primarily northern and western in distribution.

Members of the *Gnaphosa* genus have a distinctive, serrated keel on the chelicerae (see illustration, bottom left). The chelicerae, equipped with this massive keel, are used to mash the spider's prey into an unrecognizable mass, from which it sucks out all the juices—spiders cannot digest solids like we do.

You may encounter this species while camping, particularly on a gravel pad. Although it is a nocturnal hunter, it is sometimes active during the day, perhaps because it was disturbed by camping activities. This spider has been collected from under rocks, in high-tide debris on beaches, in grassy meadows and among the humid vegetation of bogs. It is found even in alpine regions.

Female epigynum (natural)

Female epigynum (cleared)

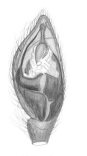

Male palp

Chelicera with serrated keel

BLACK STONE RUNNER

Zelotes fratris (Chamberlin, 1920)

Male

Female

This is a very common ground spider and is found across Canada. Its habitat covers a vast range of habitats, including forests (coniferous and deciduous), sand dunes, meadows, orchards and salt- and freshwater marshes. You are very likely to see it among the gravel of a campsite pad or in the rocks along a riverbank. Although this spider is mainly nocturnal, it can often be seen running among stones in hot sunshine.

My own observations in western Canada suggest that the male often has a bright brick red, sclerotized plate on the anterior edge of his abdomen; this is known as a scutum and is not found on the female.

These nocturnal ground spiders are handsome but are not often seen unless you look for them—it may be necessary to turn over rocks to observe them. In fact, you are more likely to see their egg sacs than the spiders themselves. These egg sacs are shaped like poached eggs and are stuck to the undersides of rocks. They have an outer flange that looks like an egg white and a domed centre that resembles a yolk. The domed area houses the spider's eggs. The whole is a beautiful pink and has the texture of parchment. These egg sacs can be found during every month of the year, though they will often be empty, the spiderlings having dispersed.

Size: *Female:* 6–8 mm

Description: carapace dark brown to black; abdomen dark brown to black

Microhabitat: on the ground under rocks or running over open ground

Distribution: British Columbia, Alberta, Saskatchewan and Manitoba

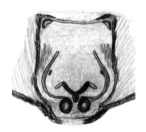

Female epigynum

Egg sac

59

MICARIA ANT MIMIC

Micaria rossica
(Thorell, 1875a)

Spider: eight legs, eight eyes, body divided into two parts

Ant: six legs, body divided into three parts, equipped with a sting, large jaws and a formic acid spray defence

Spiders in the genus *Micaria* can be found in most dry, rocky habitats. They mimic ants, and ant mimics appear in two other families of spiders in western Canada, jumping spiders (Salticidae) and money spiders (Linyphiidae). These ant mimic species are very impressive in both appearance and behaviour—they truly look and act like ants.

Size: *Female:* 4–6 mm

Description: carapace brown with longitudinal beige stripe down the centre; abdomen dark grey with horizontal white stripe

Microhabitat: on the ground under rocks; very active on hot, sunny days

Distribution: British Columbia, Alberta, Saskatchewan and Manitoba

So how does an eight-legged spider with two body parts and no antennae look like a six-legged insect with three body parts and quivering antennae? The abdomen of these spiders is indented at the sides and a white band runs between these indentations, giving the impression of a body made up of three parts. The spider also runs on just six legs and holds the first pair of legs off the ground, set a-quivering, just like an ant's antennae.

But why mimic ants? There are conflicting views as to what advantages are gained by imitating ant behaviour. An experiment was performed that involved putting an ant mimic with various larger spiders that were the ant mimic's predators, and the results suggested that something about an ant mimic helps to preserve it from attack. When it touched the ant mimic, the larger spider ran away, but if a dead ant mimic was presented, it was rapidly eaten by the predator. This suggests that it is the behaviour that protects the mimic. Ants are ferocious creatures with huge jaws, and some species can squirt formic acid at any would-be predators—a defence worth mimicking.

HOUSE WANDERER

Sergiolus columbianus (Emerton, 1917)

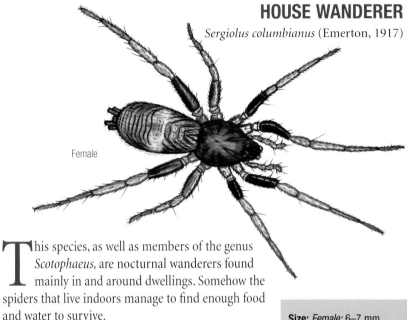

Female

This species, as well as members of the genus *Scotophaeus,* are nocturnal wanderers found mainly in and around dwellings. Somehow the spiders that live indoors manage to find enough food and water to survive.

In our own house, both genera are quite common. In the wild, they are found in pine forests among prostrate junipers and stones.

This spider is very ant-like in appearance and behaviour. The abdominal pattern consists of a broad, white, transverse band on a black background that gives the illusion of a three-part body. Also, note that the three end segments of the legs are yellow.

In an experiment, a few of these spiders were kept in captivity for observation. They would not feed on ants, only fruit flies, so mimicking ants may be a way of gaining protection by imitating a distasteful meal.

Note that the female illustrated above has a very crinkly abdomen. She had recently laid two egg sacs, and the collapse of the abdomen after this event caused the wrinkles. She died shortly after depositing the egg mass.

Size: *Female:* 6–7 mm

Description: carapace dark brown with central beige patch; abdomen black with 2 cream-coloured patches

Microhabitat: in and around houses; also in pine forests

Distribution: British Columbia and Alberta

Female epigynum

PLAIN JOE SPIDER

Orodrassus canadensis (Platnick & Shadab, 1975)

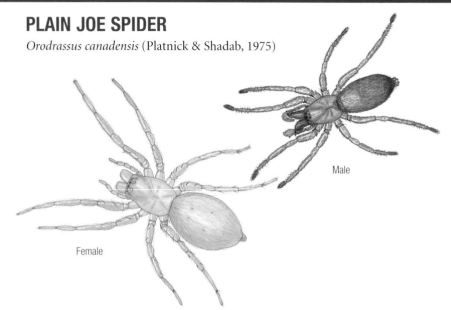

Male

Female

Size: *Female:* 9–10 mm

Description: carapace light brown or yellow; abdomen plain brown or yellow

Microhabitat: conifer forests, under loose tree bark

Distribution: British Columbia, Alberta, Saskatchewan and Manitoba

Members of the genus *Orodrassus* are rather drab-coloured, ground-dwelling hunters. These spiders are most often found in rather dry habitats such as conifer forests with spruces and lodgepole pine, fir or cedar. I have also found them on the floor of an aspen woodland; a female had built a retreat complete with an egg sac of thick, white, papery material under a fallen noticeboard, and she was fiercely guarding her eggs.

There are three *Orodrassus* species known in Canada, and the range of this genus extends as far east as Asia and eastern parts of Russia. Of the three species, the Plain Joe Spider is the most common in our region, though its range extends across Canada to the east coast.

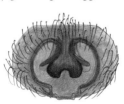

Female epigynum

Male palp

These spiders can be distinguished from other Gnaphosidae species by the male's palps and the female's epigynum, which has a median septum that is indented posteriorly. To see this, use a 20X hand lens or, better still, a microscope.

Narrow-headed Spiders
Liocraniidae

Three genera have been recorded in Canada, containing 17 species. Western Canada has six species recorded so far.

The narrow-headed spiders were once included in the sac spider family (Clubionidae) but are now placed in a family of their own.

Members of this family are ground-hunting spiders that are found under rocks and in leaf litter on the forest floor.

The common name "narrow-headed spider" refers to the narrow width of the group of eyes and the narrow labium (the lower lip under the mouth).

ORNATE FOREST SPIDER

Agroeca ornata (Banks, 1892)

Male

Size: *Female:* 6–7 mm

Description: carapace yellow or brown with black edges and paired "sun ray" marks; abdomen yellow or brown with paired dark spots or chevrons

Microhabitat: forest floor

Distribution: British Columbia, Alberta, Saskatchewan and Manitoba

This spider is quite common throughout the region. Being a nocturnal ground hunter, this species spins no web to catch its quarry, but hunts during the night for small, ground-dwelling prey. All *Agroeca* species construct a beautiful egg sac that hangs from a stalk and is camouflaged with mud. After all her work, the female abandons the egg sac to its fate.

This is an easy species to observe in captivity. Make sure you have good humidity in a narrow glass chamber, which enables better viewing, and feed the spider springtails.

Female epigynum

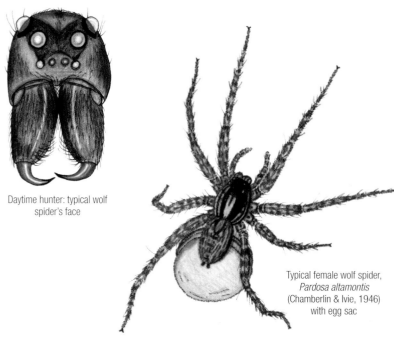

Daytime hunter: typical wolf spider's face

Typical female wolf spider, *Pardosa altamontis* (Chamberlin & Ivie, 1946) with egg sac

Wolf Spiders

Lycosidae

Thirteen genera of the family Lycosidae have been recorded in Canada, containing 101 species. Western Canada has 59 species recorded so far. All are three-clawed hunters, and most hunt during daylight hours.

Keep an eye on the ground while hiking because it is there that you will see wolf spiders. They actively hunt during hot, sunny days, and their rapid movements across the ground will attract your attention. They have very good eyesight, which they use to good effect in detecting, stalking and ambushing their prey. Wolf spiders spin no web, and most species are active nomads, even carrying their egg sacs or young spiderlings about all the time, including during the hunt.

Trochosa terricola

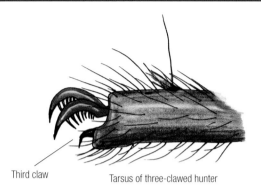

Third claw

Tarsus of three-clawed hunter

This group of spiders evolved from web weavers. This is illustrated by the possession of a third claw on each "foot." The third claw enables web-building spiders to walk and climb on their aerial webs. The Lycosidae genera that still construct webs build horizontal sheet webs and run across the upper sides just like funnel-web spiders (Agelenidae).

Wolf spiders have excellent vision that is helped by a peculiarly shaped tapetum. The tapetum is a layer of light-reflecting cells within the secondary pair of eyes and aids vision, particularly at low light levels. The tapetum reflects light, and you can highlight it at night by shining a flashlight into the spider's eyes.

Female wolf spider
carrying spiderlings on her back

NIGHT WOLF SPIDER
Trochosa terricola (Thorell, 1856)

Female

This species of nocturnal wolf spider is very stocky in build and has a rather thick body and legs. It is common throughout the region, but can be difficult to find. It is also somewhat slow moving. The Night Wolf Spider is quite secretive and prefers dark, moist microhabitats. The fangs or chelicerae carry robust teeth. This spider is most likely to be found by hand search or with a flashlight at night—you will be able to see the light reflected from its eyes. It is quite eerie to see small eyes peering at you from the darkness.

Both females and males dig a shallow scrape under a rock or log to use as a retreat during the day. It is there that the female will lay and guard her eggs until they hatch, though at times you may see her on her nightly hunt, carrying her egg sac attached to her spinnerets.

Size: *Female:* 7–14 mm
Description: carapace light brown with darker, three-forked median band; abdomen dark red with lighter red median band
Microhabitat: on the ground under rocks
Distribution: British Columbia, Alberta, Saskatchewan and Manitoba

Female epigynum

Fang and teeth

Face

NORTHERN RIVER WOLF SPIDER

Pardosa groenlandica
(Thorell, 1872)

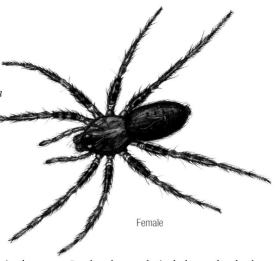

Female

Wolf spiders in the genus *Pardosa* have relatively long, slender legs and are known as "thin-legged wolf spiders." In many long-legged spider species, the body is carried high over grassy blades, the long legs making it easier for the spider to walk over the grassy canopy than to crawl between the stems. *Pardosa* is the largest genus within the family of wolf spiders; some 45 species are found in Canada. Of these, 36 species occur in our region.

Size: *Female:* 9–11 mm
Description: carapace light brown with a darker, three-forked median band; abdomen dark brown with orange median band
Microhabitat: stony riverbanks
Distribution: British Columbia, Alberta, Saskatchewan and Manitoba

The Northern River Wolf Spider is an amazing spider, capable of running very rapidly among rocks and difficult to catch. Look for this spider among the cobbled stones of dry riverbeds, along lake shorelines and even on stony marine shores. It can even hide under stones below water level, and I often wonder if it can survive underwater during spring floods when most storm channels are flooded.

If you pursue this spider with care, you may observe it seek shelter in its retreat, a silken tube leading to a small silken chamber, where it can be easily caught.

Although the epigynum of *Pardosa* species can usually be readily identified with the aid of a 10X hand lens, the male palpal organ can only be seen with a microscope.

Female epigynum

FOREST THIN-LEGGED WOLF SPIDER

Pardosa mackenziana (Keyserling, 1877)

Male

Female

This common forest species has been recorded from woodlands with both deciduous and coniferous trees, as well as from sphagnum bogs and even from the seashore among high-tide litter. It can occur in large numbers in forest habitats.

Adult females can be observed from May to September. While on a hike, you may see a female carrying a blue or white egg sac attached to her spinnerets. She can be quite conspicuous sunning her egg sac while resting on a fallen log. Or you may come across my favourite sight, a female with a fuzzy look, which is caused by a pile of spiderlings clinging to her abdomen.

You can identify the Forest Thin-legged Wolf Spider by the presence of hair-like embolus on the male's palps and lateral swellings on the female's epigynum.

Size: *Female:* 6–8 mm

Description: carapace light brown with brown median band; abdomen dark brown with light brown folium

Microhabitat: on the ground in forests

Distribution: Reported from British Columbia, Alberta, Saskatchewan and Manitoba

Female epigynum

Male palp

69

JESUS SPIDER

Pirata piraticus (Clerck, 1757)

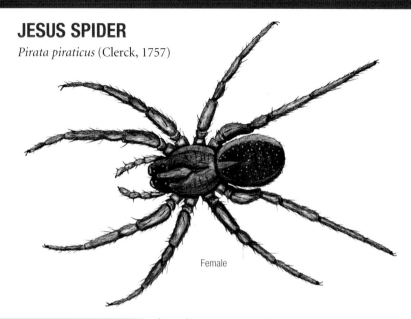

Female

Size: *Female:* 6–7 mm

Description: carapace with yellow median mark and V- or U-shaped mark surrounded by black; abdomen dark red with black chevrons, yellow or orange sides and cardiac mark

Microhabitat: surface of still water

Distribution: British Columbia, Alberta, Saskatchewan and Manitoba

This species can be found near and on water, and its ability to walk across the water's surface gives the spider its common name. When in danger, it will submerge. Like all other Lycosids, the Jesus Spider is a hunter, in this case on the water's surface, which it uses like a web. Any vibration on the surface alerts the spider to a struggling insect, and it then scoots across the water to seize its helpless victim. It can also submerge to catch prey.

Jesus Spider

There are eight *Pirata* species found in our region. This particular species is easily identified by its small size, its habitat and the V- or U-shaped mark on the carapace, as well as a yellow or orange cardiac mark on the abdomen.

Spiders in the *Pirata* genus are mostly found on lowland ponds and marshes. They build tubular retreats that go straight down through the aquatic vegetation to the water below; this is the spider's escape route. The entrance to the retreat is at the surface of the water, and the male does his courting at the retreat entrance, more by vibration than by sight.

The female creates her egg sac by first spinning a silken saucer or dish, then depositing her eggs into the dish. She

Retreat

then covers it with soft silk, followed by a tough "lid." She carries her egg sac attached to her spinnerets while hunting, and I have seen the female resting and sunning herself and her egg sac. She sometimes holds the eggs up to the sun at her tube's entrance, perhaps to help incubate them.

Female with egg sac

71

CURTAIN-DOOR WOLF SPIDER

Arctosa alpigena (Doleschall, 1852)

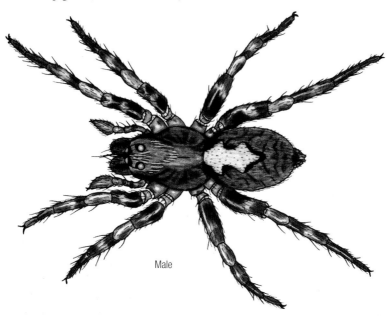

Male

Size: *Female:* 6.5–9.5 mm.
Description: carapace light brown, median band with dark brown, paired side bands; abdomen medium brown with yellow cardiac mark edged with black
Microhabitat: high-humidity habitats, sandy soils
Distribution: British Columbia and Alberta

This species is found mostly in British Columbia. It prefers humid places, where it digs a burrow and lines it with silk. It also creates a flexible curtain across the mouth of its burrow, hence the species' common name. This spider occupies a mixture of habitats, including tundra, damp pine and spruce forests and alpine meadows.

The Curtain-door Wolf Spider can be identified by the cardiac mark, which is covered in dense white hairs and surrounded by a black border. The legs are conspicuously ringed with dark bands.

This shy spider is hard to find unless you know where to look. It makes an excellent subject for the observation chamber, and with a furnishing of a carpet of moss, it will create a retreat along the glass wall, where it can be observed quite easily. The Curtain-door Wolf Spider seems to hunt at night, and it is fond of large springtails and small Harvestmen.

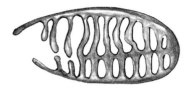

Gate-shaped tapetum of wolf spiders
(after Dondale & Redner, 1990)

Male palp showing twin claws

All wolf spiders have reflectors within their eyes. This called a tapetum, shown above. A flashlight shone at night will reflect light from the tapetum, and you will see the spider's eyes peering back at you.

In my experience, *A. alpigena* is a spider of high altitudes and latitudes and can be found in alpine, subalpine, arctic and subarctic habitats. The closely related *A. insignata* is a forest-dwelling species that replaces *A. alpigena* at lower altitudes and latitudes. In western Canada, *A. alpigena* is found in high mountain locations in British Columbia and Alberta, whereas *A. insignata* occurs at lower altitudes in the mountains and throughout the boreal forest region of Alberta, Saskatchewan and Manitoba.

Curtain-door Wolf Spider

TURRET SPIDER
Geolycosa missouriensis (Banks, 1895)

Female

Size: *Female:* 17.5–19 mm
Description: carapace orange with dark eye region; abdomen beige with black markings
Microhabitat: sandy soil
Distribution: Alberta, Saskatchewan and Manitoba

Burrow and turret

This is one of the largest spiders found in the Prairie provinces, but as far as I know, it does not occur in British Columbia. The Turret Spider, particularly the female, lives its entire life within a burrow. The burrow is most often dug in sandy soil to a depth of 10 to 25 cm (Dondale & Redner, 1990) and extends above the ground in the form of a turret. The turret is made out of surface litter that the spider incorporates into the silk of the aboveground portion of the burrow. The female sits just inside the burrow, waiting for a signal that prey is close to the turret. If you were to blow talcum powder around the turret, you would see many silk draglines or signal lines, which act as trip wires, warning the spider of approaching prey.

The males tend to be short-lived and only dig shallow burrows. Once mature, they leave their burrows forever to seek out females.

This rather robust spider is a good subject to study in an observation chamber.

Pirate Spiders
Mimetidae

Two genera of Mimetidae have been recorded in Canada, containing six species. Western Canada has three species. This is a family of araneophagous spiders that preys on other arachnids, particularly orb-web weavers (Araneidae) and comb-foot spiders (Theridiidae). Pirate spiders attack other species in their own webs, and their venom is designed to kill other spiders rapidly. They often lure the web owner by plucking the female's web in such a way as to imitate a courting male spider or a struggling prey item.

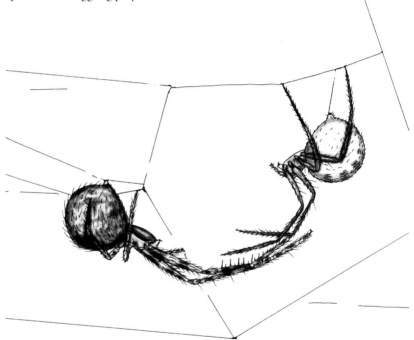

The cannibal spider (*Ero canionis*) invades another spider's web. It slowly stetches its front pair of legs over its prey, then pins it down and kills it.

CANNIBAL SPIDER

Ero canionis
(Chamberlin & Ivie, 1935)

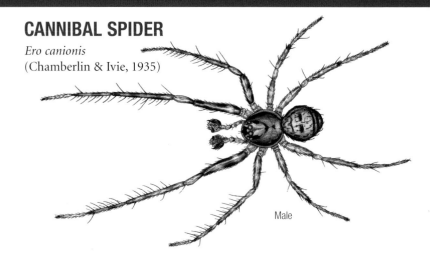

Male

Size: *Female:* 2.5–3.5 mm

Description: carapace orange edged in black, yellow head region; abdomen yellow with dark brown markings

Microhabitat: other spiders' webs

Distribution: British Columbia, Alberta, Saskatchewan and Manitoba

The Cannibal Spider preys on other spiders. At dusk, I have seen this spider quietly suspended from a thread of silk that is attached to another spider's web. It does not make a web of its own. When ready to feed, it very stealthily enters the prey's web and begins "plucking" on the strands of silk, creating vibrations that mimic captured prey or a courting male spider. The unsuspecting owner of the web will approach to investigate, and once within reach, the Cannibal Spider stealthily closes the gap between itself and its prey. Very slowly, it stretches its anterior legs out and over the prey, and then with a quick movement, it uses its legs and the spines to pin down its meal. The prey is instantly immobilized, and the Cannibal Spider then very gently bites it on the leg, paralyzing it.

Face

Mating is also a gentle affair, and the resulting beautiful egg sac is suspended from a silken stalk. Each sac contains five to eight eggs. The eggs can often be seen through the translucent white silk, which is enclosed by a latticework of wiry, golden threads. The stalk is also spun with golden threads, which are often referred to as "angel hair."

Egg sac

Lynx Spiders
Oxyopidae

Female with egg sac

One genus of Oxyopidae has been recorded in Canada, containing one species, which is found in western Canada.

This is a family of ecribellate, wandering, long-legged, daytime hunting spiders. In the field, they can be mistaken for jumping spiders (Salticidae). Although we tend to think only spiders in the family Salticidae can jump, lynx spiders are good jumpers, too, but do not have such powerful legs. They can run fast when required, and they jump onto the back of their prey items, pouncing like their namesake, the lynx.

Lynx spiders are ambush predators that prefer to sit and wait until a prey item comes within sticking distance. The many spines on their legs act as a kind of basket to aid in the successful capture of prey. These spiders also hunt actively.

LYNX SPIDER

Oxyopes scalaris (Hentz, 1845)

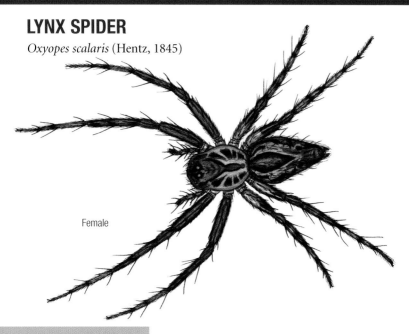

Female

Size: *Female:* 5–8 mm

Description: carapace yellow with orange, Y-shaped median mark and paired blotches; abdomen yellow with orange cardiac mark and dark blotches

Microhabitat: dry, sunny areas; low shrubs

Distribution: British Columbia and Manitoba

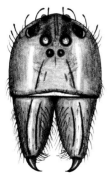

Face

So far, this is the only Oxyopidae species to be found in Canada. It is more frequent in eastern Canada; in our region, it has only been recorded in British Columbia and Manitoba. However, this is probably because of the lack of researchers. The Lynx Spider can be identified by its long leg spines and the hexagonal arrangement of the eyes (see illustration, below left).

This species prefers fairly dry, open habitats and hunts on the ground among the stems of tall grasses, herbs and shrubs. A good place to search for this spider is in dry sagebrush habitats. In British Columbia, I have collected this species in the arid area around Osoyoos.

Although this spider's eyes are smaller than those of spiders in the jumping spider (Salticidae) or wolf spider (Lycosidae) families, its eyesight is very acute, which enables it to see potential prey or a mate from some distance away.

Tree Crab or Running Crab Spiders

Philodromidae

Five genera of Philodromidae have been recorded in Canada, containing 49 species. Western Canada has 40 species.

Philodromids are tree dwellers and are very active when hunting, their surefootedness directly aided by the scopulae on the last two segments of their legs. These dense pads of hairs give the spiders a firm grip on the substrate, and they can, in fact, walk on the underside of most surfaces.

Two-clawed, tree-hunting spiders
Face of *Thanatus striatus*
(C.L. Koch, 1845)

Spiders of this family have flattened bodies, and their laterigrade legs are usually nearly equal in length and thickness. The flattened body allows the spider to creep (often sideways) under a flake of bark or into a crevice, and the side-lying legs allow it to shuffle crab-like into such places without raising the leg joints.

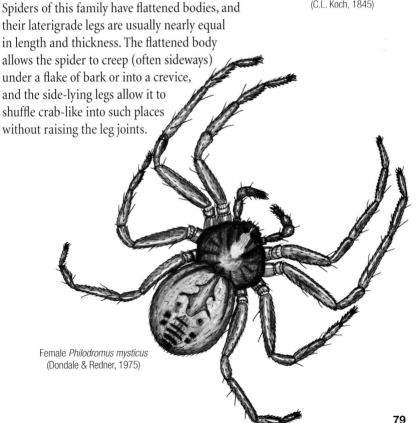

Female *Philodromus mysticus*
(Dondale & Redner, 1975)

Tree crab spiders build no web. They are active hunters capable of rapid movement. The position of the claw tufts and scopulae help these spiders make their way through tree foliage.

Most tree crab spiders overwinter as immature and subadults, maturing in late spring. The eggs are laid in early summer. In the cooler latitudes, most Philodromids have a two-year life cycle. The egg sac is most often built among the leaves or needles of these spiders' tree habitat. Some species have descended from the trees to live their whole lives on the ground, yet their body form has changed little from the arboreal design. The exception to this rule are the grass-dwelling species of the genus *Tibellus* (see *T. oblongus*, p. 82), in which modifications have evolved to assist them in their lives among the long grass stems.

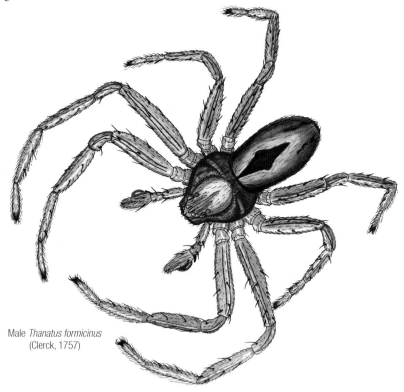

Male *Thanatus formicinus*
(Clerck, 1757)

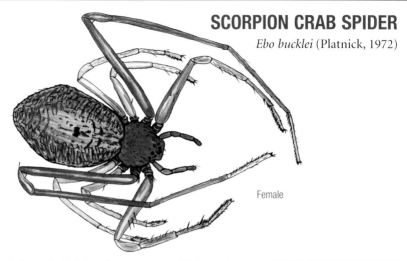

SCORPION CRAB SPIDER

Ebo bucklei (Platnick, 1972)

Female

I t is my belief that the ancestors of this species were tree crab spiders that took up the ground as a habitat. Hiding under rocks, these spiders lie in wait for their prey. My first meeting with the Scorpion Crab Spider occurred while I was collecting, on hands and knees, various grassland-dwelling spiders—I saw the tips of four "feet" protruding from under a rock, just like a scorpion waiting for its next meal. I later found a small population of this species inhabiting a rocky outcrop of layered sandstone.

Size: *Female:* 3.5–6 mm
Description: carapace red-orange; abdomen orange speckled with brown, paler mid-region
Microhabitat: grasslands; on the ground under rocks
Distribution: Alberta, Saskatchewan, and Manitoba

The legs of this family of spiders are particularly long. In most species, the legs are held flat on their side (laterigrade), enabling the spiders to shuffle sideways into narrow crevices. Their ability to do so is enhanced by their flattened bodies.

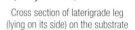

Cross section of laterigrade leg
(lying on its side) on the substrate

Philodromidae spiders are two-clawed hunting spiders and do not make webs to catch their prey. They have claw tufts and scopulae on the underside of the end segments of the legs that enable them to scale any surface, even the underside of leaves or branches.

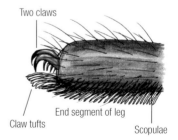

Two claws

End segment of leg

Claw tufts

Scopulae

GRASS CRAB SPIDER

Tibellus oblongus (Walckenaer, 1802)

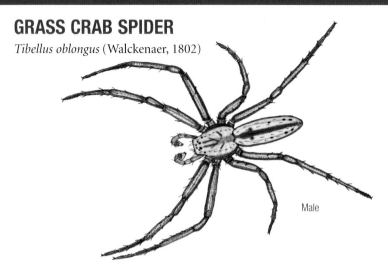

Male

Size: *Female:* 8–11 mm

Description: carapace yellow with orange, four-pronged median mark; abdomen beige with dark spots, longitudinal orange central stripe

Microhabitat: long grasses

Distribution: British Columbia, Alberta, Saskatchewan and Manitoba

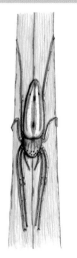

Grass Crab Spider at rest

There are six *Tibellus* species in Canada, and all six are fairly common in western Canada. *T. oblongus* is particularly common wherever there are damp, long grasses.

This grassland spider has an elongated, slender body. When at rest on a blade of grass, it can be difficult to see because it keeps its legs pressed close to the body, with two pairs in front and two pairs to the rear. The fourth pair of legs is the longest, rather than the first or second pair, which is more usual for species in this family. A beautiful stripe runs right through the dorsal surface of the body and also helps to camouflage this spider.

The egg sac is constructed at the top of a sturdy plant and guarded by the female. The spiderlings take about two years to mature.

The best way to see this spider is to catch it with a sweep net, swinging the net from side to side as you walk through the grass.

Sweep net

CARDIAC CRAB SPIDER

Thanatus coloradensis (Keyserling, 1880)

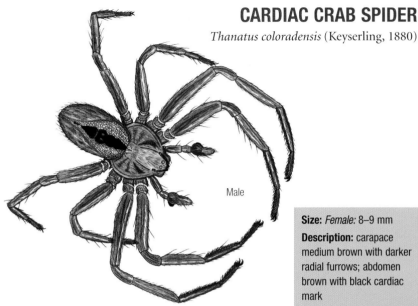

Male

Size: *Female:* 8–9 mm

Description: carapace medium brown with darker radial furrows; abdomen brown with black cardiac mark

Microhabitat: on the ground and near ground level

Distribution: British Columbia, Alberta, Saskatchewan and Manitoba

This is a ground-dwelling crab spider that is more likely to be found among the low-level field layer. It prefers the low branches of spruce trees that sweep down to the grasses along a forest edge.

This species, in my opinion, is a "lie-in-wait," ambush predator. It usually sits patiently under an object, its drab coloration blending in with the substrate. Note that, as with most *Thanatus* species, the second and fourth pairs of legs are the longest, which might enhance the spider's ability to lunge at prey. The first two pairs of legs are of equal length for catching and grasping its victims, while the fourth pair provides the thrust forward when the spider strikes at its prey.

Spiders can "amputate" one of their own legs, a process called autotomy. If a leg is held by a predator, the spider can voluntarily separate the leg at the junction of the coxa and the trochanter. The whole leg regrows within the coxa, something that I have witnessed with this particular species (see p. 84, bottom left).

Male palp

Trochanter

Point of "amputation"

Coxa

Coxa and trochanter

WESTERN APOLLO CRAB SPIDER

Apollophanes margareta (Lowrie & Gertsch, 1935)

Female

Male

Size: *Female:* 7.5–8.5 mm

Description: carapace beige with orange lines and spots, and anterior dark, V-shaped mark; abdomen brown with darker cardiac mark

Microhabitat: on the ground and among low vegetation at high elevations

Distribution: British Columbia and Alberta

This is the only *Apollophanes* species recorded in Canada. It inhabits low plants in the mountains. Very little is known about this seldom-seen species. I have tried to observe the Western Apollo Crab Spider in captivity, but it is very shy.

One of the best microhabitats in which to find this spider is among prostrate junipers that overhang a slope, such as along the edge of a trail.

One defence that spiders in general have is autotomy—spiders can amputate a leg if the leg is bitten or held by a predator. The leg regenerates inside the coxa (the segment that attaches the leg to the body). At first, the limb is small and highly folded, becoming larger and larger with successive moults.

Regeneration of new leg inside old coxa

Tarsus and metatarsus

HOUSE RUNNING CRAB SPIDER

Philodromus alascensis (Keyserling, 1884)

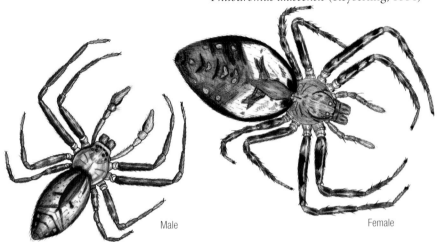

Male

Female

This species is quite common across Canada and can be found in a number of different microhabitats such as the forest floor, sand dunes, beaches and even on snow. We have found it in our camper and inside a packet of Bran Flakes (double scoop) cereal.

This is a pretty tree crab spider, with a bright orange carapace and orange-brown legs banded with yellow rings. The female is quite a bit larger than the male. The first two pairs of legs are much longer than the third and fourth pairs.

I have observed this species in captivity for some time. I watched a female build an egg sac within the scales of a spruce cone and remain outside the cone for three weeks. It is interesting that her coloration blended well with the cone. The spiderlings, once hatched, seemed reluctant to leave the safety of the cone, though they were quite active among its scales.

Size: *Female:* 5.5–6 mm
Description: carapace light orange with darker markings; anterior portion of abdomen cream-coloured, dark brown at rear and edges of abdomen
Microhabitat: coniferous and deciduous trees; frequent on buildings
Distribution: British Columbia, Alberta, Saskatchewan and Manitoba

Male palp

DISPARITY CRAB SPIDER

Philodromus dispar (Walckenaer, 1826)

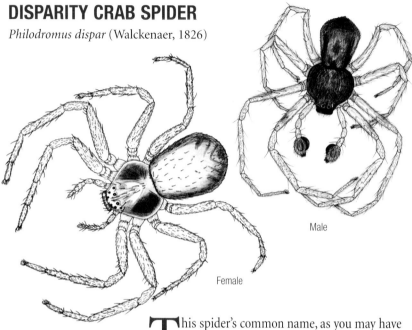

Male

Female

Size: *Female:* 5–7 mm

Description: carapace light yellow with pair of brown patches; abdomen light yellow with brown patches

Microhabitat: coniferous and deciduous trees

Distribution: British Columbia and Alberta

Female

This spider's common name, as you may have guessed, comes from the disparity in the appearance of the mature males and females of this species. The smaller male is dark red-brown, with a pale "V" mark anterior to the dorsal groove. The legs are pale yellow-brown and speckled with dark brown spots. The female much lighter in colour but is larger than the male.

This species has been recorded from British Columbia and Alberta, but it is believed to have been introduced from Europe and Asia. It is fairly common along the Pacific Coast and there is a thriving population in Waterton Lakes National Park, Alberta. Disparity Crab Spiders are found in trees, particularly spruces, but also occur in aspen and willow shrubs.

These spiders move extremely quickly among branches and foliage, hence the alternate common name, "running crab spiders," given to this genus. They can be difficult to see sometimes because they blend in with their surroundings.

VARIABLE RUNNING CRAB SPIDER (RUFUS GROUP)

Philodromus rufus (Walckenaer, 1826) and subspecies

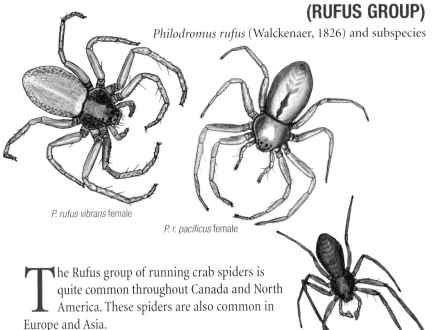

P. rufus vibrans female

P. r. pacificus female

P. r. quartus male

The Rufus group of running crab spiders is quite common throughout Canada and North America. These spiders are also common in Europe and Asia.

This interesting species and its subspecies are found across Canada, though they vary in coloration. The male in particular can be suffused with red.

Philodromus rufus has three subspecies, with intermediates, that occur in western Canada.

The definition of a species is that members can interbreed and produce fertile offspring, but they cannot mate with other species. However, subspecies can mate with other subspecies, in this case within the Rufus group, and produce fertile offspring, but they often do not interbreed in nature because of geographic isolation. However, intermediates do occur that can confuse the identification of a given spider.

Size: *Female:* 4.5–5 mm

Description: carapace yellow with paired, broad, brown-spotted lateral bands; abdomen beige with paired lateral bands of orange spots

Microhabitat: coniferous and deciduous trees

Distribution: *P. rufus* is common across Canada and throughout the Northern Hemisphere; *P. r. quartus* is common across Canada; *P. r. pacificus* occurs in western Canada; and *P. r. vibrans* is found in eastern Canada.

Fishing or Nursery-web Spiders
Pisauridae

Two genera of Pisauridae have been recorded in Canada, containing seven species. Western Canada has two species recorded so far.

This family of spiders is generally regarded as semi-aquatic. The common name "nursery-web" for these spiders is related to the tent-like web that the female creates. When the egg sac is close to hatching, the female builds a huge structure among the tall grasses. She places her egg sac inside the tent and remains on guard outside until she dies. Meanwhile, the spiderlings emerge from the sac and begin moving around inside the protection of the nursery web. These tents can be a common sight in midsummer. The larger ones are usually made by *Pisaurina* species (found in eastern Canada) and the smaller ones by *Dolomedes* species.

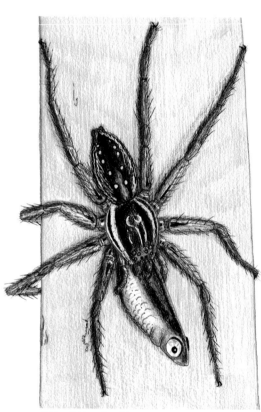

Fishing Spider with catch

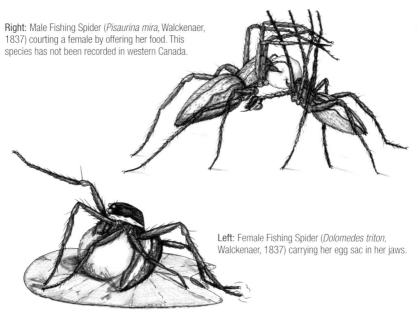

Right: Male Fishing Spider (*Pisaurina mira*, Walckenaer, 1837) courting a female by offering her food. This species has not been recorded in western Canada.

Left: Female Fishing Spider (*Dolomedes triton*, Walckenaer, 1837) carrying her egg sac in her jaws.

When the male approaches a female, he must do so with caution. Careful courtship is necessary to persuade the female that he is not her next meal, but the father-to-be of her spiderlings. Pisauridae males have an endearing way of doing just that. First the male catches a prey item and wraps it up into a silken parcel. Holding the present in his jaws, he approaches the female. Once she has accepted his gift and begins to feed, he will mate with her. It has been observed that in the absence of prey, the male will wrap up a fragment of some sort and present that to the female, but this is cheating!

Dolomedes triton

Dolomedes triton and dragonfly

FISHING SPIDER

Dolomedes triton (Walckenaer, 1837)

Female

Size: *Female:* 13–20 mm

Description: carapace orange or dark with paired, white, longitudinal bands; abdomen dark with two lines of white spots

Microhabitat: on and around still water

Distribution: British Columbia, Alberta, Saskatchewan and Manitoba

The genus *Dolomedes* comprises wetland spiders that hunt actively during the daytime. They are often found around the edges of still water, where they hunt among the emergent vegetation and also on the water's surface. These spiders do not construct a web to snare their prey, but use the surface tension of water as a web. You can often see them resting on floating vegetation with their first and second pairs of legs extended across the water's surface, waiting for the vibrations of a struggling insect trapped in the surface film of the water. Once prey has been detected, the spider skates across the surface, snatches up the prey and returns to its resting station. These spiders have also been observed catching fish in this way—from the surface, not by diving for them. When disturbed by a would-be predator, the Fishing Spider submerges to escape. It does this by crawling down the stem of an emergent plant.

Female

Members of the Pisauridae family are fairly large spiders with long, robust legs, and when skating across the water, they sink quite deeply into the surface film. They have large eyes and good vision and are easily disturbed. In fact, if you walk along a shoreline, you will often cause this species and pirate spiders (*Pirata* spp.) to skate out across the water.

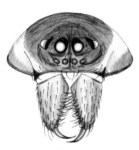

Face

Female

Jumping Spiders
Salticidae

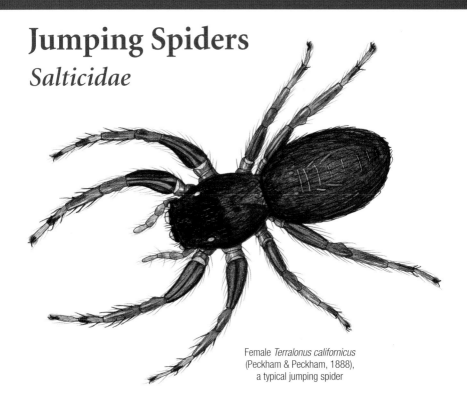

Female *Terralonus californicus*
(Peckham & Peckham, 1888),
a typical jumping spider

Face of *Salticus striatus*

Thirty-four genera of Salticidae have been recorded in Canada, containing 107 species. Western Canada has 62 species recorded so far.

Jumping spiders spin no snare but actively hunt their prey down by sight, and they have very good eyesight. For example, if you are watching a jumping spider and you move to one side, it will move its body so as to keep you in its field of vision. It will observe you with its four large, forward-facing eyes, often raising its carapace to get a better look.

Jumping spiders are extremely active on warm sunny days and are able to leap onto the back of their prey, hence their common name. They can jump from one substrate to another, but before leaping across the gap, they create a safety line by attaching a silken thread to the substrate.

Jumping spiders are great favourites among naturalists owing to their bright colours and endearing ways. If you wish to study one for a while, keep it in a glass enclosure. They are easy to feed and observe. Introduce a small mirror and watch the displays this spider can produce.

Courting male

The above illustration is one of my favourite pieces of art—it portrays a male jumping spider displaying to a female. He will perform a particular dance, which is unique to his species, along with a semaphore language of leg movements. Each species has its own "language" of dance.

ZEBRA JUMPING SPIDER

Salticus scenicus
(Clerck, 1757)

Female

Male

Size: *Female:* 5–7 mm

Description: carapace dark grey with white, X-shaped mark; abdomen dark with white bands across abdomen

Microhabitat: outside walls of buildings

Distribution: British Columbia, Alberta, Saskatchewan and Manitoba; introduced from Europe

This introduced species likely arrived with humans and their furniture, and it has established itself throughout the region. You will most likely see it hunting on the outside wall of your house, particularly on a hot, sunny day.

Female epigynum

Male palp

Unlike the previous spider drawings, which were created using a microscope after the spiders were immersed in alcohol to bring out their colours, the Zebra Jumping Spiders that you see with the naked eye appear black and white, hence their common name. (There is a difference between a living spider's coloration and the same specimen displayed in alcohol.)

Notice the much-enlarged chelicerae, or jaws, of the male. These are used in sparring contests between rival males. The equally elongated male palps are distinctive and aid the male in reaching the female's epigynum with safety.

Female face

Male face showing chelicerae

This species is readily identified in the field with the aid of a 10x hand lens. Using the characteristics illustrated here, you should be able to make an identification.

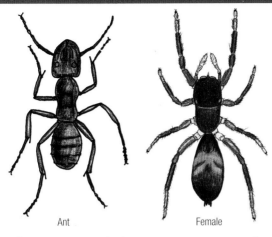

Ant

Female

ANT MIMIC JUMPING SPIDER

Synageles canadensis
(Cutler, 1987)

S trangely enough, this genus mimics ants, and so do genera in two other families of spiders, the stealthy ground spiders (Gnaphosidae) and a few species of money spiders (Linyphiidae). But why? These ant mimic species are very impressive in both appearance and behaviour because they really do look and behave like ants.

"Normal" jumping spider

Somehow, an eight-legged spider with two body parts and no antennae makes itself look like a six-legged insect with three body parts and quivering antennae. How? The carapace of these spiders is indented at the sides and a white band runs between these indentations, making the

Size: *Female:* 3.5–4 mm

Description: carapace dark brown; abdomen medium brown with a cream-coloured, X-shaped mark

Microhabitat: in hot sunshine among ants

Distribution: British Columbia and Alberta

body look as if it is divided into three parts. The spider also runs on just six legs and holds the first pair off the ground so they look like an ant's antennae. Why these spiders have taken the trouble to adapt in this way is unknown.

There are conflicting views as to what advantages are gained by mimicking ants. When an ant mimic is put with various larger spiders—the ant mimic's worst enemies—the results suggest that there is something about the ant mimic that helps to preserve it from attack. If the larger spider touches a live ant mimic, the predator will run away, but if a dead ant mimic is given to the larger spider, the prey is rapidly eaten. Based on this information, it is possible that the ant mimic's behaviour protects it. Ants are ferocious creatures with huge jaws, and some species can squirt formic acid at any would-be predators. Looking like an ant may be a sound defence strategy.

RED-BACKED JUMPING SPIDER

Phidippus johnsonii (Banks, 1895)

Male

Female

Size: *Female:* 7–12 mm

Description: carapace dark mauve; abdomen bright red with darker cardiac mark

Microhabitat: among rocks at high altitudes

Distribution: British Columbia and Alberta

Male

Female

Male palp

This is a fairly common jumping spider that occupies relatively dry habitats such as coastal dunes and dry forests. Both the male and female have a bright red abdomen; in addition, the female also has a black central stripe on the abdomen. The rest of the body is mostly black.

This is one jumping spider species that mimics mutillid wasps (or velvet ants, as they are commonly known), and these spiders possess a very painful bite. The Red-backed Jumping Spider only bites when threatened, but being bitten results in swelling and pain at the injury site that lasts for several days, so be careful.

This spider hunts fairly large prey and has been known to feed on other spiders.

The female constructs a retreat under a heavy rock. On finding her, the male will cohabit for a time. He is typically found lodged under a "flysheet" attached to the female's main retreat and egg chamber. Instead of making an egg sac, the female spins a shallow bowl of silk in which she lays her eggs, then adds a "lid" and fastens the whole thing to the wall of her retreat.

Male

Female

SNOW SPIDER

Chalcoscritus carbonarius
(Emerton, 1917)

This is an unusual jumping spider. Most other members of the Salticidae family are gaily coloured, and this is the only one I know of that is jet black. Also, it has only been observed at altitudes above 1800 metres in regions that are geographically and climatically extreme for this family.

I believe that Emerton first recorded this species in 1917 in southern Alberta. It has since been found in only a few places in Montana and Alaska at high altitudes.

I located this species in 2003; it was a rather large population occupying a small area beside a high tarn. Permanent snow fed the small lake, and during the month of September, I found all stages of the spider's life cycle: mature males and females, egg sacs and spiderlings. This was surprising because the area was under snow for seven months per year, at least. Are these spiders active through winter? We still don't know.

It is my belief that this species is a remnant from the past ice age, and that its black coloration is an adaptation to conserve heat from whatever light falls on it, even under the snow.

Size: *Female:* 2.5–4 mm
Description: carapace black; abdomen dark grey
Microhabitat: edges of high-altitude tarns
Distribution: Alberta

Face

97

COYOTE JUMPING SPIDER

Euophrys monadnock (Emerton, 1891)

Male

Female

O nly this single species of this genus has been recorded in my database for western Canada. The two sexes of this spider are very different in their behaviour and general appearance. The male is entirely a nice shiny black, whereas the female is dull grey or beige.

Size: *Female:* 6–7 mm

Description: carapace dull grey or beige with dark eye region; abdomen medium brown with dark lines and chevrons

Microhabitat: under rocks and among low vegetation

Distribution: British Columbia, Alberta, Saskatchewan and Manitoba

The male is a rather active hunter on the ground, whereas the female hunts under the slabs of rock that dominate their habitat.

Jumping spiders get their name from their ability to jump well. Other spiders such as wolf spiders, sac spiders and lynx spiders are able to jump, but not to the extent that Salticids can. The common name for this species, Coyote Jumping Spider, relates to the male's coyote-like pounce following the careful stalking of a prey item.

In this species, the thrust for the takeoff comes from the third pair of legs. Just before it leaps, the spider fastens a safety line to the substrate, then it pulls the first two pairs of legs close to its body and launches itself out and up. The force of the jump comes from an increase in hemolymph (blood) pressure and the sudden relaxation of the leg muscles.

Male palp

The female illustrated above is a "spent" female. The wrinkles on her abdomen are the product of laying a mass of eggs. Afterward, the abdomen shrinks, hence the wrinkles.

HAIRY FLAG JUMPING SPIDER

Habronattus hirsutus
(G. & E. Peckham, 1888)

Male

The genus *Habronattus*, the flag jumping spiders, are among my favourite of the jumping spiders (Salticidae). It is a large and diverse genus restricted to the New World. Canada has about 16 species recorded, and 13 of these can be found in our region. They occur in warm habitats, such as those on southern or eastern aspects, often on the stony shorelines of big lakes.

In this particular species, the male has a "flag" of long, black hairs. The leg segments are bright blue, and the face, chelicerae and femurs of the first pair of legs are bright orange—a beautiful sight to present to the female.

The highly ornamented males seem to prefer washed-up logs on which to perform their striking courtship dance. The dance is like a language or "semaphore speech," and each species has a language that is different from other species. Based on my observations, it is possible that sound is involved as well, in the form of drumming, which may be amplified by the hollow log!

These spiders are truly beautiful to look at under the microscope.

Size: *Female:* 4–7 mm
Description: carapace dark brown fading to light brown posteriorly; abdomen medium brown with lighter lines
Microhabitat: on the ground
Distribution: British Columbia and Alberta

Face

Leg of male

FLAG JUMPING SPIDER

Habronattus oregonensis (G. & E. Peckham, 1888)

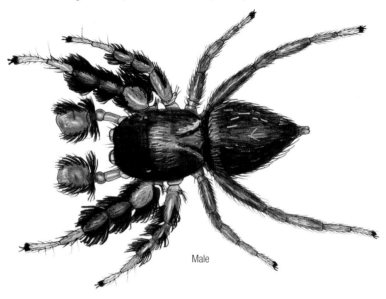

Male

Size: *Female:* 4–6 mm

Description: carapace light brown with dark eye region and posterior, and inverted, V-shaped mark; abdomen dark brown with cream-coloured anterior crescent

Microhabitat: lakeside among beached logs

Distribution: British Columbia and Alberta

Jumping spiders are the darlings of the arachnology world, and this particular species is a favourite of ours. It is fairly common in various habitats, but one that stands out is that of a natural lake's shoreline, especially where beached logs are common. The reason is that the male prefers to court the female on top of a log, making the pair particularly conspicuous. Not only does the male carry out his dancing display in this open site, but he also drums on the log for added effect.

Front leg of male showing "flag" hairs

I only wish that our readers could observe the male and his dance because it is a sight never to be forgotten. However, if you capture a male and place him front of a mirror, he may dance for you.

FEATHER FLAG JUMPING SPIDER

Habronattus cuspidatus
(Emerton, 1917)

Male

W
e believe that we heard this male spider before we saw him, though neither of us can be sure. We were camping on the banks of Kootenay Lake in British Columbia when a faint sound drew my attention to a washed-up log a few feet away. There I noticed a beautiful male spider "drumming" on the log. He was easy to see because of his rapidly vibrating, bright orange palps.

Size: *Female:* 4–6 mm
Description: carapace dark brown with lighter X-shaped mark; abdomen black with two grey crescents and cardiac mark
Microhabitat: warm, stony ground
Distribution: Alberta and Saskatchewan

Male palp

As Platnick (1971) showed us, a male jumping spider has two alternative types of courtship at his disposal. Each consists of distinctly different motor patterns and involves different sensory channels. If the male encounters a female outside her nest, he uses Type 1 courtship, which relies on visual displays. Type 2 courtship occurs if the male encounters a female inside her nest. All male jumping spiders display their specific dance in front of a female. I like to think that this form of courtship is similar to a sign language, and every species seems to be unique.

Can you decipher this message from a courting spider?

YELLOW-LEGS JUMPING SPIDER

Pelegrina flavipedes (G. & E. Peckham, 1888)

Male

Female

The genus *Pelegrina* is quite common in western Canada, and these spiders are particularly found among the foliage of spruce trees. The architecture of the dense branches and needles of conifers makes them a favoured hunting ground for many spider species.

Size: *Female:* 4–6 mm
Description: carapace orange with dark eye region; abdomen yellow with dark chevrons and blotches
Microhabitat: conifer forests
Distribution: British Columbia, Alberta, Saskatchewan and Manitoba

The male Yellow-legs Jumping Spider has conspicuous white and brown stripes. The sides of the face are also striped with white, and three white spots can be seen on the "forehead." The female has a brassy sheen to the abdomen.

Male

The male's palps and the female's epigynum are quite conspicuous even without a 10X hand lens.

Male palp

Face (drawn after Wayne Maddison)

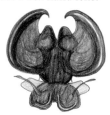

Female epigynum

PEPPERED JUMPER

Pelegrina galathea (Walckenaer, 1837)

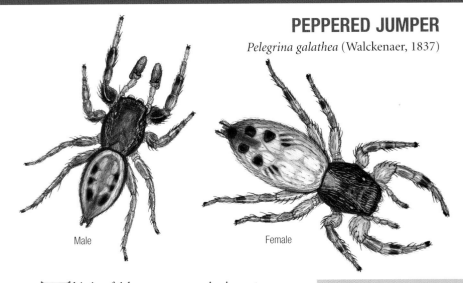

Male

Female

T his is a fairly common species in eastern Canada; in our region, it is found only in Alberta. It prefers warm, exposed sites, and I often collect this spider from the lower field layer, particularly by sweeping prostrate junipers.

Size: *Female:* 4–7 mm
Description: carapace dark brown; abdomen beige with yellow and black spots
Microhabitat: sunny, short grasslands
Distribution: Alberta

Male palp

Jumping spiders have superb eyesight, and although they usually have eight eyes, the eyes are structurally divided into two different types: main eyes and secondary eyes. The main eyes are always the anterior median eyes and often appear dark. The secondary eyes have light-reflecting layers (the tapetum) inside that reflect the light of your flashlight so the eyes seem to glow.

Normal epigynum

Normally in this book, I have illustrated the female's epigynum as one would see it on an intact specimen. For identification, it is often necessary to clear the area (make it transparent) to see the internal structure (see illustrations, right). To identify a given species it is beneficial to have both sexes in hand.

Cleared epigynum

Spitting Spiders
Scytodidae

This is a family of six-eyed haplogyne spiders typically found in the tropics. Only one genus has been recorded in Canada, containing two species, and only one species is found in western Canada.

Spitting spiders are quite rare this far north, and I have only encountered them in the warm, humid building of a fish hatchery on Vancouver Island. These spiders have also been reported in Ontario, where they are only found in people's houses, particularly old, established buildings.

The spider with a "machine gun"

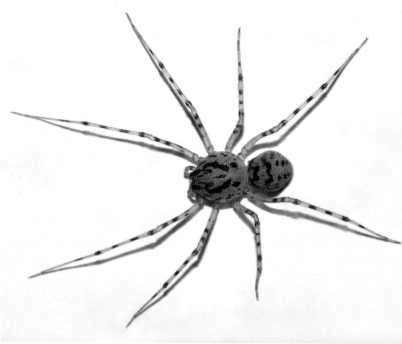

Scytodes thoracica, female

SPITTING SPIDER

Scytodes thoracica (Latreille, 1804)

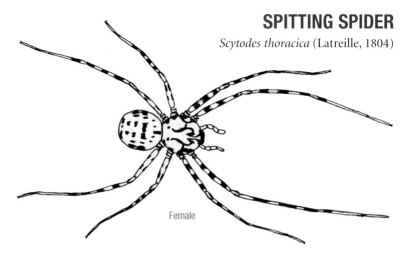

Female

I have included this species because it illustrates one of the many marvellous adaptions that spiders possess.

Size: *Female:* 4–6 mm
Description: carapace yellow with black markings; abdomen yellow with black markings
Microhabitat: buildings with warm, humid interior
Distribution: British Columbia

The Spitting Spider has a highly characteristic domed carapace that houses a pair of two-lobed glands. The front lobe produces venom, and the rear lobe produces a gummy glue. The lobes are connected by ducts to the openings near the tip of each fang. The spider is capable of shooting this combined poison and glue at its prey, literally sticking it down to the substrate and subduing it at the same time.

This is a very secretive, nocturnal spider that has a particularly slow, measured walk. One good identifying characteristic for the species is that the carapace and the abdomen are both the same size, and in our region, it is only found in British Columbia in old buildings with a warm, humid interior.

The female is sometimes seen carrying a bundle of eggs in her jaws, the eggs barely held together by a few strands of silk.

Spitting Spider
"shooting down" a fly

105

Violin or Brown Spiders
Sicariidae

One genus has been recorded in Canada, containing two species. Western Canada has one species recorded so far.

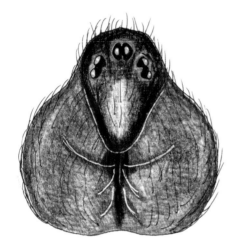

Violin Spider's carapace

Compare to
a violin

VIOLIN SPIDER

Loxosceles laeta
(Nicolet, 1849)

Male

This is a notorious spider owing to its potent venom, and its bite has been blamed for many cases of poisoning. The venom has a toxic effect on human cells; it produces wounds and persistent sores, though seldom death.

The Violin Spider prefers desert-like habitat similar to its native habitat in Central and South America. This species is included here because many people ask about it, but be reassured that it is not native to Canada. The only records are from Vancouver, British Columbia.

This is a six-eyed, haplogyne spider with a rather flattened body, and it is capable of quickly burying itself under sand. Its flattened body also allows the spider to squeeze into narrow cracks among rocks, which it lines with silk to create a retreat. The retreat is supplied with trip lines of silk that extend across the rock face and are capable of ensnaring prey items. The Violin Spider is a generalized feeder, eating whatever it can catch.

"Haplogyne" refers to a primitive form of sexual apparatus. The female has internal copulatory organs, and the male has relatively simple palps. In more advanced species, the females have external, sclerotized epigyne and the males have more complex palps.

Size: *Female:* 5–13 mm
Description: carapace medium brown with darker eye region and fovea; abdomen dark grey
Microhabitat: arid areas and mesic forests
Distribution: British Columbia; introduced from Central and South America

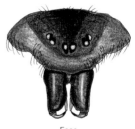

Face

107

Crab Spiders
Thomisidae

Misumenops asperatus

Seven genera of Thomisidae have been recorded in Canada, containing 62 species. Western Canada has 47 species recorded so far.

This is a family of ambush predators. Many species are ground-dwellers that lie in wait for their prey to literally walk into their outstretched two pairs of forelegs. Crab spiders are very sturdily built, with rather flattened bodies and strong, laterigrade legs. Their whole locomotion is crab-like, hence their common name. Most are mottled in drab earth colours suitable for their way of life. Examples are found in the genera *Xysticus* and *Ozyptila*.

Representatives of the *Misumena, Misumenoides* and *Misumenops* genera are called "flower crab spiders." Their policy is to sit in a flower and wait with outstretched legs for any would-be pollinators. These spiders are mostly decked out in bright colours such as yellow or white with a splash of red.

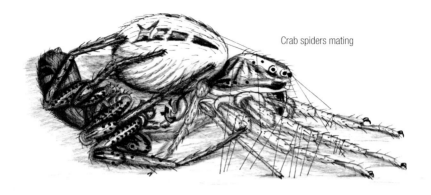
Crab spiders mating

Members of the genus *Tmarus* try to convince any potential prey that they are a twig or bud. These spiders sit very still, pressed tightly against a twig, making them almost impossible to see, and snap up any insect that chooses to walk along that twig.

Misumena vatia

Because it is very dangerous for the male to court a female, the male is very cautious in his approach. Once close enough, the male will tie the female down to the substrate with strands of silk, and once she is secured, he proceeds to mate with her. There is not a lot of choice for the female, and she usually mates with the first male that comes along. Once mated, she is able to break free of her bonds.

Flower Crab Spider with prey

FLOWER CRAB OR GOLDENROD CRAB SPIDER

Misumena vatia (Clerck, 1757)

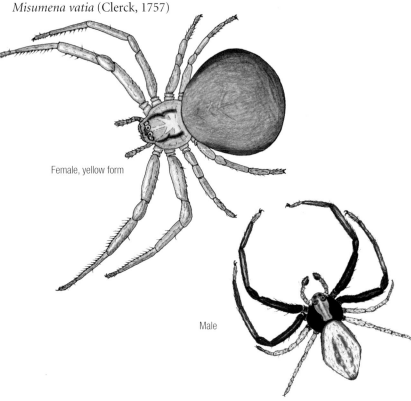

Female, yellow form

Male

Size: *Female:* 9–11 mm

Description: carapace white or yellow with parallel red or orange; abdomen white or yellow with parallel red stripes at the edges

Microhabitat: in flowers

Distribution: British Columbia, Alberta, Saskatchewan and Manitoba

The Flower Crab Spider is a lie-in-wait, ambush predator. Being possibly the laziest spider in the world, it spins no web, but just sits in a flower with its arms outstretched, waiting for its next meal to walk into its mouth, so to speak. Crab spiders get their common name from the arrangement of their legs and the way they shuffle around just like a crab.

The females are generally bright yellow or white with bright orange or red lateral markings. Surprisingly, a spider with these bright colours becomes almost invisible within its chosen flower. If it happens to choose a flower of the wrong colour, the spider can change to white or yellow, but no other colour.

Among the petals, the spider sits and waits for its prey. The two pairs of front legs are very long and curve inward, somewhat like those of a crab. In this position, the spider lies perfectly still until a large bee, bumblebee or butterfly practically walks headfirst into its legs, which then grasp the prey. Next, the spider sinks its fangs into the neck of its victim. Venom is pumped through the hollow fangs into the prey and digestion begins. Spiders cannot take in solids, so all food must be reduced to a liquid form outside the spider's body before ingestion can occur.

Female, white form

Female, white form

Male, yellow form

Female, yellow form

TOAD CRAB SPIDER

Ozyptila gertschi
(Kurata, 1944)

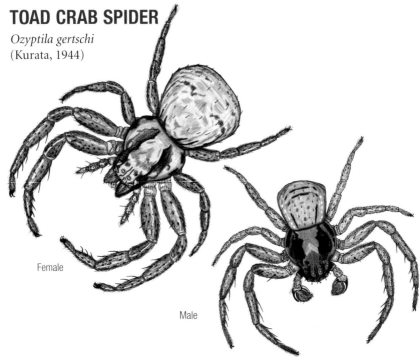

Female

Male

Size: *Female:* 3–4 mm

Description: carapace light brown with two dark brown parallel bands; abdomen light brown with dark brown blotches

Microhabitat: on the ground among stones and vegetation

Distribution: Alberta, Saskatchewan and Manitoba

Spiders of the genus *Ozyptila* are, to my mind, just like diminutive toads. Their niche is that of ambush predators, and all they do is lie quite flat to the substrate and wait for a passing meal. Unless it moves, this spider is hard to see, even if one is sitting right in front of you. The body is very flattened and circular, while the legs are short, stout and laterigrade (lying on their sides). Twelve *Ozyptila* species occur in Canada, but in western Canada we have just six.

To mate with the female, the male Toad Crab Spider binds the female down with a fine mesh of silk, often known as a "bridal veil" (see illustration, top of p. 109).

At egg-laying time, the female creates a silken saucer in which to deposit her eggs. The saucer is then covered with a lid of silk to form a lenticular egg sac. Next, the female spins a protective outer covering of more silk. She stands guard over the egg sac until the spiderlings emerge, then she dies.

PIRATE CRAB SPIDER

Xysticus emertoni (Keyserling, 1880)

Female

Male

O f the approximately 40 *Xysticus* species that are found in Canada, western Canada has 34 species recorded so far. This species is one of our largest and is also the most common.

I have often found this spider lodging inside the folded leaf of an unrelated species' retreat that houses a developing egg sac, and I've actually watched it eating the hatchlings, hence the common name I have given it, Pirate Crab Spider. Very few true spiders have common names, but I feel that the general public appreciates common names.

Although the female is rather drab, the male is a handsome fellow, with his dark red-brown carapace flecked with off-white. His legs are dark red-brown also, while the cardiac mark on the abdomen is a pleasing shape. Owing to this spider's size, it should be possible to identify it in the field. If you turn the male over and view the palps, you will observe that the tibia has a long, pointed "spike" and a long, pointed "heel."

Size: *Female:* 7–8 mm

Description: carapace light brown with darker brown markings; abdomen beige with brown chevrons

Microhabitat: on the ground and among herbaceous plants

Distribution: British Columbia, Alberta, Saskatchewan and Manitoba

Male palp

113

OVIFORM CRAB SPIDER

Xysticus ellipticus (Turnbull, 1880)

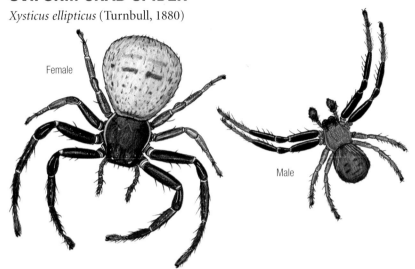

Female

Male

Size: *Female:* 4–5 mm

Description: carapace orange with yellow borders; abdomen yellow with orange blotches

Microhabitat: on the ground among forest leaf litter

Distribution: British Columbia, Alberta, Saskatchewan and Manitoba

Female epigynum

Elliptical spermathecae

This colourful species is a woodland spider that lives among the leaf litter of the forest floor. The male is very small compared to the female. Also, the male's first two pairs of legs are a conspicuous black colour. This illustrates the importance of display male spiders—be recognized or be eaten. You are very likely to find this spider by installing a pitfall trap or by searching the forest leaf litter.

The species name *ellipticus* refers to the spermathecae, which are elliptical in outline (see illustration, below left). Observe the difference between the epigynum, which is the female's external opening, and the internal spermathecae, which is a storage pocket for sperm. The female can keep the sperm alive in her body for an extended period of time, until she decides to lay her eggs, at which time the sperm and eggs are mixed.

TRIANGLE CRAB SPIDER

Xysticus triangulosus (Emerton, 1894)

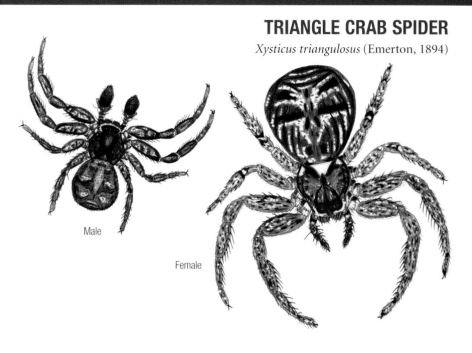

Male

Female

One might think that this spider's common name refers to the distinctive shape of the abdomen, but Emerton named the species for the small, triangular ridge, called the tegulum, near the centre of the male's palp. This spider is a ground dweller in high subarctic and alpine meadows.

The complex male palps of this species and most other entelegyne spiders have a series of hard and soft parts. The soft parts can be inflated and allow the palpal organ to expand hydraulically during mating. The tegulum is one of a number of sclerites, or hard parts. As the hydraulic pressure of the male's "blood" expands the palp, the sclerites become erect and engage with the female's epigynum. This holds the palp secure while mating takes place. It is a "lock and key" kind of union, each organ having evolved in step with the other.

Size: *Female:* 7–8 mm

Description: carapace dull red with dark lateral bands; abdomen red-brown with many white and black lines and blotches

Microhabitat: on the ground under rocks

Distribution: British Columbia, Alberta and Manitoba

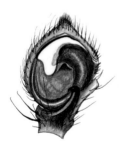

Male palp

115

ELEGANT CRAB SPIDER
Xysticus elegans (Keyserling, 1880)

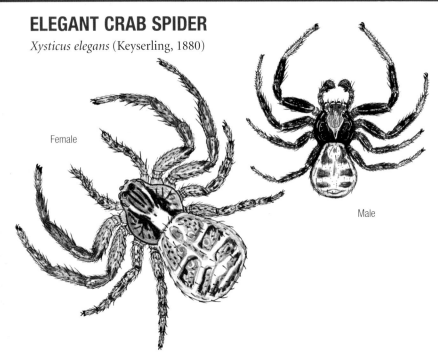

Female

Male

Size: *Female:* 8–9 mm

Description: carapace pale red-brown with pale median area; abdomen light brown with paired brown bars separated by white lines

Microhabitat: on the ground and among flowering plants

Distribution: British Columbia, Alberta, Saskatchewan and Manitoba

Cow parsnip
(*Heracleum sphondylium* ssp. *montanum*)

This species is common throughout Canada. There are about 200 *Xysticus* species known in the world.

This particular species of crab spider is found among leaf litter and under stones. This may be a reflection of capture techniques—the easiest way to collect spiders is with the aid of pitfall traps, which only really sample ground-dwelling species. This spider may also be found in other microhabitats.

My local population of the Elegant Crab Spider, which is in southwestern Alberta, has adopted the life of a Goldenrod Crab Spider (pp. 110–11). I can always find this spider among the flowers or seeds of woodland cow parsnip, admittedly only during the plant's flowering season. I have come to believe that this lifestyle is confined to the second year's generation. As with the Flower Crab Spider, each generation appears to adapt to a different plant or plants.

WEB-WEAVING SPIDERS

TRUE SPIDERS: WEB WEAVERS

In the previous section, we dealt with true spiders that hunt for their prey. In this section, we will look at some of our region's web-weaving spiders. For a general description of true spiders, please refer to pp. 41–43.

Funnel-web Spiders
Agelenidae

There are about 52 Agelenidae species contained in 15 genera in my records for Canada. Some 36 species have been recorded in western Canada.

Species in this family spin a tubular tunnel or funnel in their sheet web that extends downward and acts as an escape route when the spider is threatened. The spiders run across the upper surface of this sheet of silk to catch prey. In some species, an aerial superstructure of knockdown threads is built above the sheet web. An insect that hits these lines falls down onto the sheet, then the spider sprints out to grab the prey, bite it and drag it back to its retreat for consumption.

Typical sheet web with funnel retreat

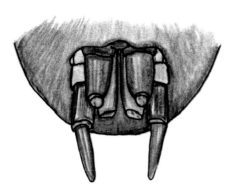

Posterior spinnerets are longer than the anterior ones
and have two segments.

The majority of species in this family have posterior spinnerets that are clearly longer than the anterior ones and have two segments. The males generally resemble the females but have a slimmer body and much longer legs. One characteristic of most Agelenidae species is a row of long hairs, called trichobothria, on the legs. The hairs increase in length toward the end of the leg segment, and at the end of the leg, you will find the three claws of a web-spinning spider.

Some of the species listed here can be identified in the field with a 10X hand lens. Other species will require higher magnification.

Trichobothria on first segment of leg

GIANT HOUSE SPIDER

Tegenaria gigantea (Chamberlin & Ivie, 1935)

Female

Face

Spiders of the genus *Tegenaria* are the most likely to be found within your house. The male Giant House Spider is perhaps Canada's largest spider and has a leg span of 10 cm. You may find the male in your bathtub; he often gets trapped there when he is drawn to water to drink. Sightings of this spider are particularly frequent during the latter half of the year. At this time, the male is mature, having left his web for good in search of a female.

Size: *Female:* 11–16 mm

Description: carapace light brown or orange with dark markings; abdomen beige with paired dark blotches

Microhabitat: in or near buildings

Distribution: British Columbia, Alberta and Saskatchewan; introduced from Europe

Female

The Giant House Spider builds a large, often dusty-looking sheet web high up among the rafters or in the crawl space beneath a house, preferring an overhang of some sort. The web has a tubular tunnel retreat at one end that gives it a funnel-like appearance. This tunnel is where the spider takes its prey after it's been captured and where the spider rests and sleeps. The female also hangs up her egg sac for safekeeping there. The far end of the tunnel is open and curved downward, creating an escape route.

Like most spiders, this one possesses quite potent venom to subdue its prey. This species is not known to harm humans.

The Giant House Spider was introduced to Canada during the early 1900s and has strongly increased in numbers since then.

HOBO SPIDER
Tegenaria agrestis (Walckenaer, 1802)

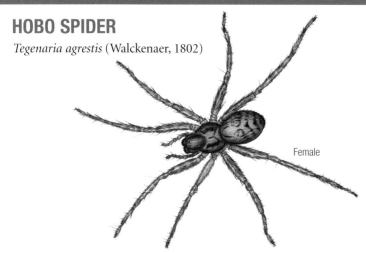

Female

Size: *Female:* 10–15 mm

Description: carapace dark red with a pair of black bands; abdomen beige with black chevrons

Microhabitat: on the ground under rocks and logs

Distribution: British Columbia and Alberta

Male palp

Female epigynum

As the species name *agrestis*, meaning "land, fields or countryside," implies, this spider normally lives in the countryside, particularly under rocks or rotten logs, away from human habitations. However, in the colder months, it has been known to move into houses and will bite humans with little provocation. Although this spider has had bad press, its venom is not as harmful as some would have us believe. I personally have been bitten twice with no harmful effects.

The Hobo Spider's funnel web is usually attached to the side of a rock, and the funnel and its escape route lead under the rock. If you look closely at the web, you will notice a number of vertical threads of silk. These are known as "knockdown lines." Any flying creature that collides with these strong silken lines will be knocked down onto the web, and the spider, alerted by the impact, will rush out of the funnel and subdue the intruder. This arrangement reminds me of my youth in England during World War II. We lived in what was known as "Bomb Alley," and our defence was to fly "barrage balloons," which supported strong wires to snare incoming bomber planes.

The Hobo Spider is similar in general appearance to the Giant House Spider (p. 121). It can only be identified positively by examining the sex organs (illustrated above).

GRASS FUNNEL-WEB SPIDER

Agelena utahana (Chamberlin & Ivie, 1935)

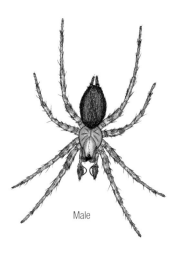

Male

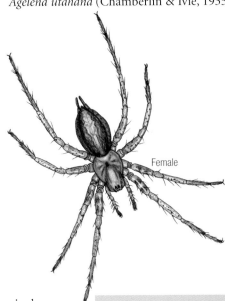

Female

This grassland and woodland species has conspicuously longer spinnerets than the previous species of the family Agelenidae. If you have an opportunity to watch this spider repairing its web, note how agile these spinnerets are.

To watch any spider in its natural habitat, use a pair of binoculars. I suggest that you sit about 3 metres away and, with the aid of your pooter, fire (deliver) a prey item into the spider's web and watch. The spider (usually a female in a conspicuous web) will come rushing out of her funnel and attack the prey, paralyzing it instantly with one bite. She will then drag it back to her retreat and start to feed. If you wish to catch this spider to take a closer look, you must first very gently place a plastic jar or tube directly in front of the escape tunnel, then chase her down the funnel and into the jar or tube.

One place to observe funnel-web spiders is alongside gravel roads, where a fine layer of dust will reveal the webs.

Size: *Female:* 7–10.5 mm

Description: carapace rich brown; abdomen dark brown with cream-coloured central band

Microhabitat: grasslands and woodlands

Distribution: British Columbia, Alberta, Saskatchewan and Manitoba

Female

123

WESTERN FUNNEL-WEB SPIDER

Novalena intermedia (Chamberlin & Gertsch, 1930)

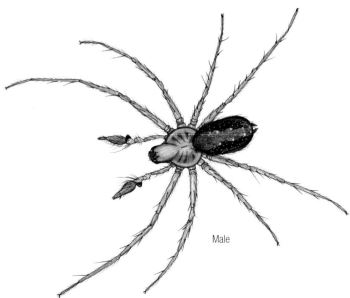

Male

Size: *Female:* 7–10 mm

Description: carapace light brown with dark radial furrows; abdomen black with red central band

Microhabitat: in and around buildings

Distribution: British Columbia and Alberta

Male palp

The male of this species is striking and easily identified in the field. I have found this spider along the Pacific Coast, particularly the Sunshine Coast area. A good place to look for it is in and around old abandoned buildings or under wood planks lying on the ground. Search for it in the summer, particularly for the male, who leaves his web in search of a female. The male will live with the female for some weeks before she eats him.

This species makes a non-sticky sheet web, complete with a funnel, which is the spider's retreat and the place in which the female deposits her egg sac. The sheet of silk can be quite large. When collecting this species, remember that the "funnel" is also an escape route, so look for the end of the funnel and watch it when disturbing the web.

This spider prefers to build its web close to an overhead structure, so crawl spaces are a good place to look for it.

Blue-silk Spiders
Amaurobiidae

Five genera of Amaurobiidae have been recorded in Canada, containing 14 species. Western Canada has 10 species

This family is interesting in that it includes both cribellate and ecribellate forms, so within this family, species either have a cribellum or this organ may be absent. One hypothesis is that the cribellum is an ancient organ that has been lost many times throughout the evolution of spiders.

Face

Blue-silk spider's web

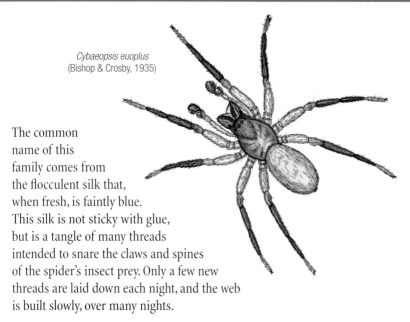

Cybaeopsis euoplus
(Bishop & Crosby, 1935)

The common
name of this
family comes from
the flocculent silk that,
when fresh, is faintly blue.
This silk is not sticky with glue,
but is a tangle of many threads
intended to snare the claws and spines
of the spider's insect prey. Only a few new
threads are laid down each night, and the web
is built slowly, over many nights.

Cribellum

The silk threads arise from the cribellum plate just
in front of the spider's spinnerets, which in this family
are divided into two sections. The cribellar area is
densely covered with many tiny spigots. In one species,
40,000 spigots have been counted. These delicate
spigots produce extremely fine silk threads, just
0.01 µm thick (for reference, 1 µm is one micrometre,
one millionth of a metre, or one thousandth of a millimetre). These extremely
fine threads are "combed" out of the cribellum with rhythmic movements of the
calamistrum, a row of comb-shaped hairs situated on the metatarsi of the fourth
legs. This combing produces dense "wool," which is probably more efficient for
catching prey than threads with beads of glue because it doesn't deteriorate so
quickly.

The tripping threads extending out from the retreat have obvious structure
and are arranged to snare crawling forms of prey. Once the prey has become
entangled, the spider typically bites a leg of the victim and then drags the meal
backward into its retreat.

Calamistrum

AVALANCHE SPIDER

Callobius nomeus (Chamberlin, 1919)

Male

Female

This species creates tunnels of silk among coarse scree slopes and avalanche falls. Fresh silk at the entrance of the tunnels appears bright blue but fades with age. This species will also make its web within a cavity in the bark of a tree trunk. Web spinning is usually carried out at night.

If you shine a flashlight at the entrance to the web's tunnel, you can often see the spider's eyes reflecting back at you. This is caused by a layer of light-reflecting crystals, called the tapetum, in the eyes. This also gives the secondary eyes a lighter colour than the other six.

The male of this species has quite elaborate palps, which can be seen with the aid of a 10X hand lens.

I collected a female from a rock fall and cared for her in an observation chamber. She laid an egg sac that produced a number of spiderlings. After a couple of months of caring for her brood, she died, and the spiderlings fed on her body, a mass of small spiders sucking out her juices.

Size: *Female:* 9–11 mm

Description: carapace rich brown with black head region; abdomen light brown with dark edges, medium brown cardiac mark and chevrons

Microhabitat: loose, deep layers of rocks

Distribution: British Columbia, Alberta, Saskatchewan and Manitoba

Male palp

127

HACKLE-BAND SPIDER

Amaurobius borealis
(Emerton, 1909)

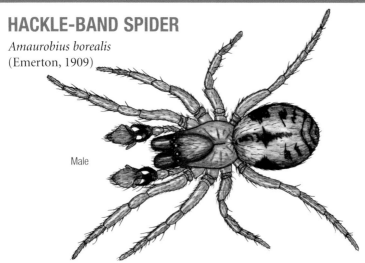

Male

Size: *Female:* 4.5–6 mm

Description: carapace orange with dark eye region; abdomen beige with dark brown cardiac mark and paired blotches

Microhabitat: rock and bark crevices

Distribution: British Columbia, Alberta, Saskatchewan and Manitoba

Male palp

You may find this species among stacked timber or logs. Look for a circular retreat inside a crevice and the characteristic meshed web on the surface surrounding the entrance. The freshly laid-out silk will have a bluish tinge and a lace-like appearance. This spider is not uncommon in houses, particularly in damp basements.

The Hackle-band Spider's prey is mostly pedestrian insects that crawl near the web. You can provide a prey item for the female and watch her eat it. She nearly always bites a leg of her victim, then drags her struggling meal across the web that surrounds her retreat.

As previously mentioned (see p. 42), cribellate spiders do not add beads of glue to the silk of their webs. The silk is combed out of a special plate of hundreds, sometimes thousands, of spigots, all producing silk. In this way, the dry hackle-band, or wool-like mass of silk, is made. This type of web has the advantage that even in damp conditions, it is still very active because the tangle of silken threads entraps insects by becoming entangled with the insect's legs and/or spines.

All blue-silk spider species are nocturnal web spinners, so visiting a hackle-band web at night, armed with a flashlight, is a good way to observe this spider.

Orb-web Weavers
Araneidae

Seventeen genera of Araneidae have been recorded in Canada, containing 56 species. Western Canada has 38 species.

The orb web: beautiful in its design and engineering

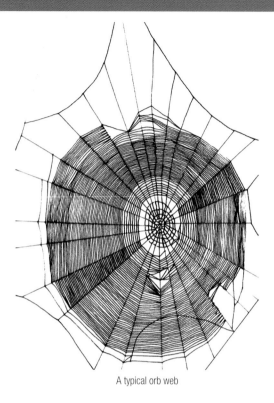

A typical orb web

The orb web, in its delicate beauty, is an engineering feat of economic design. The central hub is constructed of fine, non-sticky silk on which the spider rests, head downward, waiting for its next meal during the hours of darkness. The catching section of the web is a spiral of silk studded with droplets of glue.

During the day, the spider hides in a retreat. You can often find the spider by tracing back the signal line that runs from the centre of the web to the retreat. The whole web is suspended from a bridging line. To begin its web, the spider wafts a line of silk into the wind until it snags a nearby twig. From this bridging line, the spider constructs the framework and the radial threads, which are like the spokes of a wheel. The silk from which the web is made is very high in protein and "costs" the spider dearly. For this reason, the spider recycles the used silk each day by eating the old web before its spins a new one.

The following Araneidae species are those that you are most likely to come across. The best way to find these spiders is to look for their webs. To do this, look into the sun, and if you get the angle right, the sunlight will pick up the shining silk. Don't forget that the web is meant to be invisible.

NOTCH-WEB SPIDER

Zygiella nearctica (Gertsch, 1964)

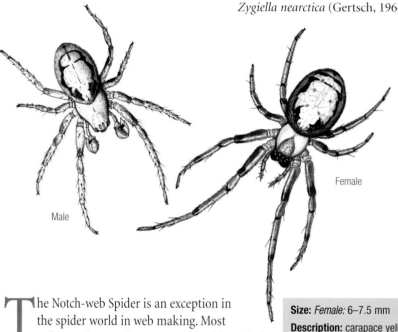

Male

Female

The Notch-web Spider is an exception in the spider world in web making. Most web-weaving species construct a sticky, spiral snare on a framework of radiating lines. Think about this—it is much easier for a spider to keep going around and around in a continuous circle to lay down the spiral. However, when laying down the sticky silk, the Notch-web Spider stops near the top of the web, turns around and goes back the way it came. This requires a complete change in behaviour. It is my suggestion after a number of observations that this style of web construction gives the spider the option to run over either the front or the back of the web to reach its prey.

The Notch-web Spider's retreat is at the apex of the "notch." One of the radii acts as a "telephone wire," alerting the spider when its next meal has crashed into the web, allowing the spider to almost fall down onto its prey item.

Size: *Female:* 6–7.5 mm

Description: carapace yellow with brown head region; abdomen with central yellow area bordered in black and edges a rich brown

Microhabitat: shrubs

Distribution: British Columbia, Alberta, Saskatchewan and Manitoba

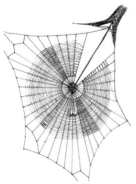

Notched web with retreat

131

CAT SPIDER

Araneus gemmoides
(Chamberlin & Ivie, 1935)

Female

Face

Size: *Female:* 14.5–18mm

Description: carapace yellow; abdomen yellow with brown blotches

Microhabitat: outdoor buildings and window frames

Distribution: British Columbia, Alberta, Saskatchewan and Manitoba

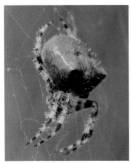

Female

The large Cat Spider is a common sight during fall, particularly outside our windows or near a light. Children in western Canada have given this spider its name—the two "humps" represent the ears of a cat, and the body pattern, I am told, resembles the face of a cat.

These are the spiders we love best for their beautifully constructed orb webs. In this case, the central hub of the web is closed, filled in with a lattice of silk. The spider sits on the hub, and when it feels the vibrations of a struggling insect, rushes down and deals with the prey item.

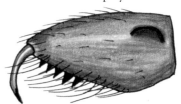

Fangs and teeth

Orb-web spiders generally have strong teeth on their chelicerae, and prey is chewed and mashed up with digestive juices. The end result is a pellet of insect remains that you may find on a window ledge. These "leftovers" are different from the near-perfect, sucked-out husks left by comb-foot (Theridiidae) and crab (Thomisidae) spiders.

Courtship involves the male serenading the female by plucking on her web, which results in her adopting the mating position. After mating, the male usually manages to escape and avoid being eaten, so he can subsequently mate again. In some species, the female starts to eat the diminutive male during mating, and this occurs as a normal practice among spiders.

Female Cat Spider from below

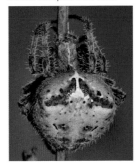

Female

Orb web with dew

ORCHARD SPIDER OR SIX-SPOTTED ORBWEAVER
Araniella displicata (Hentz, 1847)

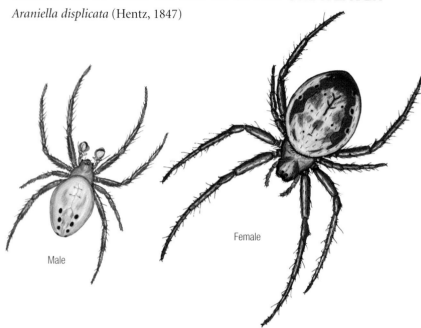

Male

Female

Size: *Female:* 5.5–7mm
Description: carapace orange or yellow; abdomen yellow with red border and black spots
Microhabitat: shrubs
Distribution: British Columbia, Alberta, Saskatchewan and Manitoba

Female

This spider is variable in its colour scheme; the main colour is yellow or orange with some red occasionally thrown in. The paired black spots at the rear of the abdomen plus a small red spot just above the spinnerets are good identifying marks for the genus *Araniella*.

The common name for this spider comes from fact that it is most often found in fruit trees. It spins a small orb web that is often confined to the underside of a single leaf. The orb structure can be very eccentric, with many of the threads arranged in a rather haphazard fashion.

The female builds a large, woolly, straw-coloured egg sac, which she covers with leaves. She will remain on guard over it until she dies. When the leaves fall in autumn, the egg sac ends up on the ground, where it remains until spring. When the weather warms up, the emerging spiderlings climb the tree or shrub, and the cycle repeats itself.

BRIDGE SPIDER OR FURROW ORBWEAVER

Larinioides cornutus (Clerck, 1757)

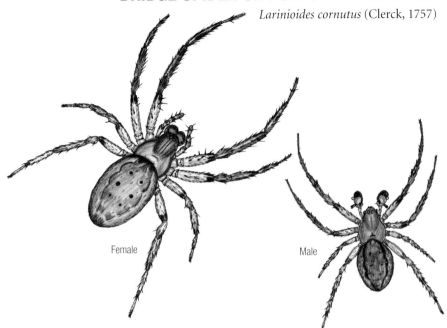

Female

Male

Species of the *Larinioides* genus most often spin their orb webs near water, and this particular species is often found on and around bridges. It also occurs frequently along the coast among rocks and piers, and does not seem to be bothered by the salt.

The Bridge Spider can be identified with the aid of a 10X hand lens. Both the female's epigyne and the male's distinctive palps can be seen this way.

The spider's retreat is usually above the web on the underside of the structure. You will find a fine line of silk leading from the web's hub to the retreat. The female creates a tough, papery, silky retreat that is open at both ends, offering a possible escape route if the spider is attacked—even the fiercest predators can fall victim to other hunters. Spiders' main enemies are other spiders, such as pirate spiders (Mimetidae). A number of wasp species also hunt spiders.

Size: *Female:* 9.5–11 mm

Description: carapace orange with dark eye region; abdomen medium brown with paired spots and lines

Microhabitat: near water

Distribution: British Columbia, Alberta, Saskatchewan and Manitoba

Male palp

135

TRASHLINE SPIDER
Cyclosa conica (Pallas, 1772)

Female

Male

Size: *Female:* 5–6 mm

Description: carapace dark brown; abdomen light brown with an anterior white, inverted V-shaped marl

Microhabitat: moist woodlands

Distribution: British Columbia, Alberta, Saskatchewan and Manitoba

Female epigynum

One web you may notice, nearly invisible as it may be, is that of the Trashline Spider. The vertical white line (stabilimentum) that crosses the web makes it conspicuous. There is a gap at the web's hub where the spider sits day and night quite camouflaged. The "trashline" is made of silk and gets its name from the remains of past meals and egg sacs that are woven into its upper area. This spider's web is most often found in woodland areas, particularly among dead twigs near shoulder height.

Other spiders also construct a stabilimentum in their webs. It is the zigzag silken line that goes through some webs. It is found particularly among spiders in the hackle-band orbweaver family (Uloboridae). These other types of stabilimentum vary in design from circles to an X-shape. It is not known for sure what advantage the stabilimentum gives the spider. Some of the reasons could be a means of hiding (camouflage) or a way to protect the web from larger animals than the usual prey by making it more visible.

Notice the pointed rear abdomen of this species, which makes identification of this spider easy in the field.

Trashline Spider hiding in web

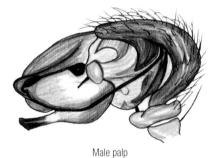

Male palp

Trashline web

Cyclosa conica

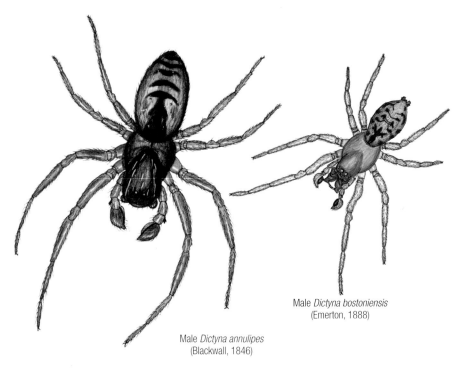

Male *Dictyna bostoniensis*
(Emerton, 1888)

Male *Dictyna annulipes*
(Blackwall, 1846)

Mesh-web Spiders
Dictynidae

Seven genera of Dictynidae have been recorded in Canada, containing 53 species. Western Canada has 42 species.

This is a family of cribellate or hackle-band spiders. Its species spin silk fluffed up with a comb to produce "hackle-bands" that entangle prey.

Many species in this family are specialized troglodytes that live in deep forest litter and under bark and rocks. Their webs are reduced sheet webs that function primarily as retreats and are nearly invisible.

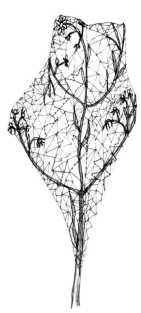

Mesh web

138

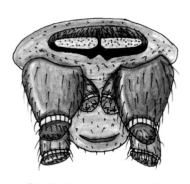

The cribellum (spinning plate) produces
the hackle-band of silk.

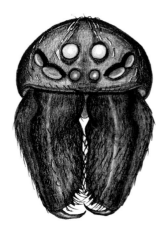

Dictyna face

Some mesh-web spiders are arboreal, building webs above the ground among foliage, dead flowers and dried stalks, and also among branch endings in spruces. The web is formed by an irregular mesh, an almost ladder-like line of hackled (i.e., tangled and woolly) silk. The silk is not sticky; there is no glue involved. The maze of silk entangles the leg spines of the spider's insect prey and slows down its escape. One advantage of this type of silk is that it works even when wet.

Mesh-web spiders are small but are made conspicuous by their webs, which are often spun high in a dead flowerhead. On a damp morning, the webs show up like jewelled socks threaded over flower stalks. Each web is made up of a square, ladder-like pattern, giving the members of this family another common name—ladder-web spiders. The web is a permanent structure that is added to on a daily basis, with each new addition having a faint bluish look.

Many *Dictyna* species are not easy to identify in the field owing to the fact that the abdomen patterns are composed of fragile hairs that are easily rubbed off.

The calamistrum on the hind legs "combs out" the silk.

139

WESTERN MESH-LADDER SPIDER

Dictyna major (Menge, 1869)

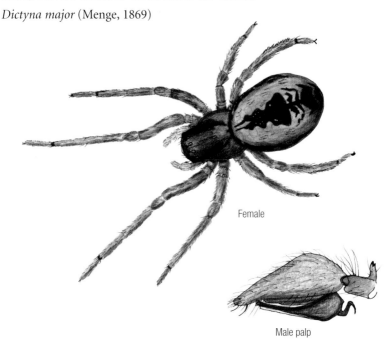

Female

Male palp

Size: *Female:* 2–4 mm

Description: carapace brown with two parallel bands; abdomen beige with dark folium cardiac mark

Microhabitat: low vegetation

Distribution: British Columbia, Alberta, Saskatchewan and Manitoba

Female epigynum

Although this is a small species, its web can be conspicuous. It is built low to the ground, usually around a dead flowerhead, and looks like a tangled mat.

Although most spiders are strict predators and live alone, the two sexes of this species often share the same web, living together but feeding separately.

During courtship, the male first vibrates his legs against the web to attract the female's attention. He then seizes her chelicerae, or jaws, with his special, elongated jaws. His long jaws probably help prevent him from becoming the female's next meal.

ALBERTA MESH-WEB SPIDER

Lathys alberta (Gertsch, 1946)

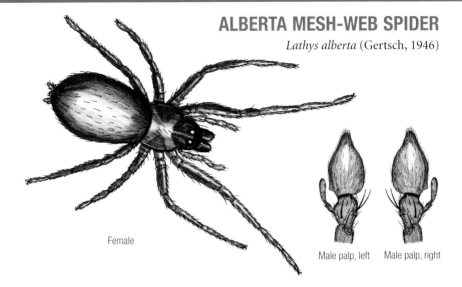

Female

Male palp, left   Male palp, right

Size: *Female:* 2.5–4 mm

Description: carapace brown with darker head region; abdomen yellow edged with dark brown

Microhabitat: tall-grass flower stems

Distribution: Alberta and Manitoba

Male palp ectal view

Male palp ventral view

When out hiking or camping, take the time to stop and stare. Look around you. Many hikers often just walk, and maybe the only opportunity they take to look at the invertebrate life is when they stop to eat lunch.

Examine tall-grass flower stems or any dead flower stalks. If you look closely, you may see a tangled mesh web clothing the dead flowerhead. The spider responsible is very likely to be a favourite species of mine, the Alberta Mesh-web Spider. It is a favourite because the male and female live together quite happily—for a while, at least. The female often ends up eating her mate eventually.

If you're sitting under a spruce tree, look up at the outmost twigs of needles—they may be covered with fine silk. These small branches of needles form a bottlebrush-like arrangement that is suitable microhabitat for a number of spider species. They form a protective cover for the spider and her mesh web, which will ensnare a variety of wandering insects.

141

Six-tailed Spiders or Small Sheet-web Weavers
Hahniidae

Three genera of Hahniidae have been recorded in Canada, containing nine species. Western Canada has eight species.

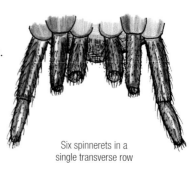

This is a family of small sheet-web spiders, so small that their webs are usually built across a depression in the ground or between stones. This group used to be included with the funnel-web spider family (Agelenidae), but owing to

Six spinnerets in a single transverse row

a number of differences, these species have been put in their own family. One of their unique characteristics is that small sheet-web spiders build no retreat to the web. They are found most often at high altitudes in montane and lower subalpine ecoregions.

Very little is known about the biology and life of the spiders in this family. I have included them here as a matter of interest.

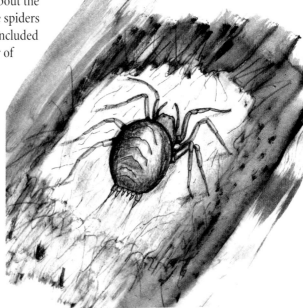

Six-tailed spider

SIX-TAILED SPIDER

Hahnia arizonica (Chamberlin and Ivie, 1942)

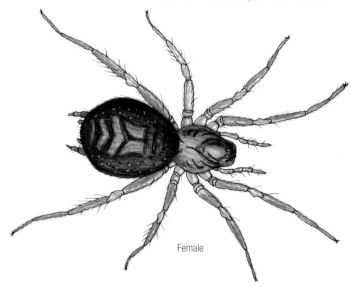

Female

This species is widespread throughout North America, from Texas to Alaska. It is a three-clawed, web-weaving spider that can be recognized by the spiracle opening, which is twice as far from the epigastric furrow as from the base of the median spinnerets. This spider's distinctive transverse row of six spinnerets means that you are unlikely to confuse it with any other species.

The Six-tailed Spider can be found in a range of different habitats, and its web may be embedded among moss or leaf litter at quite a depth, even as deep as 2 metres below the scree of a rock fall. Its web is quite small, less than 4 centimetres across, and lacks a retreat or funnel. You are likeliest to see the web when it is covered with dew. Although this species reportedly does not build a web in captivity, I have observed it to do so.

Size: *Female:* 2.0–2.5 mm

Description: carapace brown; abdomen dark brown with chevron markings

Microhabitat: under slabs of rock and among leaf litter

Distribution: British Columbia and Alberta

Male palp

Female epigynum

143

Dwarf Sheet-web Weavers
Linyphiidae

This family may be the largest in the Northern Hemisphere, with more than 3500 species. One hundred and twenty-nine genera have been recorded in Canada, containing 509 species. Western Canada has 398 species in 100 genera.

Web of Filmy-dome Spider (*Neriene radiata*, Sundevall, 1930)

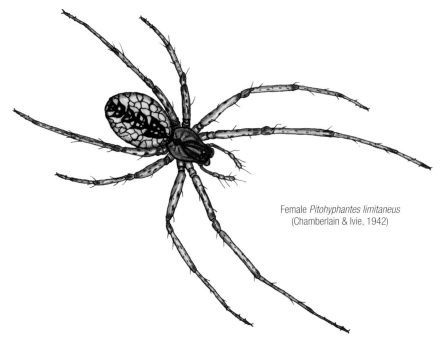

Female *Pitohyphantes limitaneus*
(Chamberlain & Ivie, 1942)

The majority of the species in this family are very small spiders that build hammock webs, usually on the ground or among the field layer. These spiders run along the underside of their webs and can be confused with the comb-foot spiders (Theridiidae), which also run across the web underside, so take care with identification.

Some of the larger sheet webs made by members of the genus *Linyphia* have a superstructure of hanging lines above the sheet. This tangle of threads acts as a group of knockdown lines. Insects hitting these lines fall onto the sheet of silk and are attacked from below by the spider.

Out of this vast collection of species, we have chosen a few that may come to your attention owing to their larger size (sheet-web weavers) or to their particular type of web (money spiders), though many species and their webs are very small.

Head and face of male
P. limitaneus

145

CUP-AND-DOILY SPIDER

Frontinella pyramitela (Walckenaer, 1841)

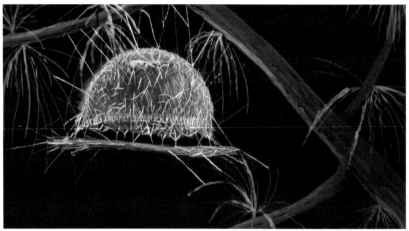

Cup-and-doily Spider web

Size: *Female:* 3.5–5.6 mm

Description: carapace medium brown with dark brown, U-shaped mark; abdomen white with dark bands and spots

Microhabitat: low bushes

Distribution: British Columbia, Alberta, Saskatchewan and Manitoba

The Cup-and-doily Spider's web is very conspicuous. This small spider weaves a fairly complex sheet-web system that consists of an inverted, dome-shaped web, or "cup" (sometimes referred to as a "bowl"), suspended above a horizontal sheet web, or "doily," hence the species' common name. The web of the Cup-and-doily Spider requires a particular structure of supports: a fork in which to spin the cup and an overhanging branch from which to hang the knockdown threads.

The knockdown lines impede the flight of small insects so that they fall onto the cup. The spider hangs from the underside of the cup and bites through the web at any small flies, gnats or other insects that fall down onto the non-sticky webbing.

This species' webs are commonly seen in damp forests. They become visible if you get the sun in the right position. In late summer, they often contain both a male and a female spider—like many dwarf sheet-web weavers, both genders of this species may cohabit for some time.

FILMY-DOME SPIDER

Neriene radiata (Walckenaer, 1841)

Male

Female

This spider spins a remarkable domed web with a superstructure of fine threads that is very conspicuous when seen against the sunlight. The web is most often observed among the forest field layer and is often called a "filmy-dome web," which gives the species its common name. The spider hangs from the underside of the web, and when a prey item falls onto the sheet of silk, it bites a hole in the web and pulls its meal through to the underside.

I have often found this spider among the very large boulders of rock falls. The web is strung across the cave-like opening between boulders, most often at the upper reaches of the "cave." In one instance, the spider's prey was baby cave crickets. I also found the rare *Arcuphantes fragilis* (Chamberlin & Ivie, 1943)— a species with no common name—in the lower reaches of the same site.

The male's palps are quite complex (see illustration, bottom right), which to me begs the question, has sexual selection gone haywire in this species?

Size: *Female:* 3.5–6.5 mm

Description: carapace yellow or dark brown; abdomen yellow with brown cardiac mark

Microhabitat: low vegetation and among rocks

Distribution: British Columbia, Alberta, Saskatchewan and Manitoba

Female epigynum

Male palp

147

SPRUCE HAMMOCK SPIDER

Pityohyphantes cristatus (Chamberlin & Ivie, 1942)

Carapace

Head of male

Female

Size: *Female:* 4–6 mm

Description: carapace beige with tuning-fork-shaped mark; abdomen with purplish brown folium edged with yellow

Microhabitat: lower branches of conifers

Distribution: British Columbia, Alberta and Saskatchewan (Cypress Hills)

Female epigynum

Male palp

This species is easily identifiable in the field with the aid of a 10X hand lens. The carapace has a tuning-fork-shaped mark, the prongs of which are broad and barely separated. The femurs have black spots, while the abdomen displays a purplish brown folium (leaf-shaped mark).

The female's epigynum has a spoon-like projection at its centre line (see illustration, left). The male's palp is quite complicated and beautifully designed to transfer sperm to the female's spermathecae, where it is stored until egg-laying time.

This spider's sheet web is typicaly found on the lower branches of conifers, particularly spruces. The web sags and is shaped like a hammock, hence the species' common name. As with all Linyphids, this spider lives its life hanging from the underside of the web. It feeds on small gnats and midges that rise out of the surrounding grass or go to rest in the foliage of the trees.

Similar species, *Pityohyphantes costatus* and *P. subarcticus,* are found in the parkland and boreal forest regions of Alberta, Saskatchewan and Manitoba.

LASSO MONEY SPIDER
Microlinyphia mandibulata (Emerton, 1882)

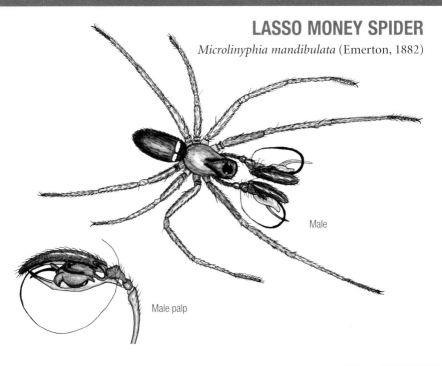

Male

Male palp

There are five species of *Microlinyphia* that are fairly common throughout western Canada. It is the peculiar, looped adaptation of the male's embolus, a tube that delivers sperm, that gives this species its common name.

The Lasso Money Spider constructs a typical Linyphiidae web—a horizontal sheet web under which the spider hangs upside down throughout its life. When flying insects hit the overhead scaffolding of threads, they are knocked down onto the web's upper surface, then the spider bites through the web and pulls the prey item to the underside, where it is devoured.

Generally, it is very dangerous for a male spider to attempt to mate with a female— the female typically eats the male during the mating process. In this species, the male adapts his "reach" by elongating his chelicerae and embolus so that he can stay out of harm's way and mate safely.

Size: *Female:* 3.5–5.5 mm
Description: carapace orange with dark, V-shaped mark; abdomen brown with two white bars anteriorly
Microhabitat: low vegetation
Distribution: Alberta, Saskatchewan and Manitoba

Male, side view of head and body showing elongating carapace, chelicerae and embolus

149

FLYING MONEY SPIDER

Erigone dentipalpis
(Wider, 1834)

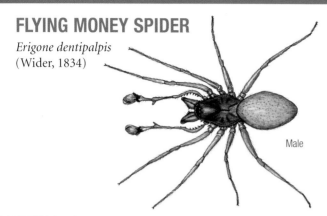

Male

Size: *Female:* 1.5–2 mm
Description: carapace dark brown or black with toothed edges; abdomen plain grey
Microhabitat: low vegetation
Distribution: Alberta

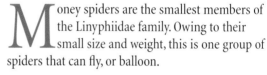

Male palp

Money spiders are the smallest members of the Linyphiidae family. Owing to their small size and weight, this is one group of spiders that can fly, or balloon.

Ballooning is a method of dispersal. The spider lets out a strand of silk into the air, and even a gentle breeze will lift the spider up so it "flies." At certain times of the year, many millions of money spiders use this method to move to new areas. This is how spiders occasionally get caught in people's hair. It was thought that when this happened, the person would come into money, hence the common name "money spider."

A money spider preparing to "fly"

This species builds a tiny, delicate sheet web at ground level, often within a small depression in the substrate. It builds no retreat but hangs from the underside of the web. If alarmed or attacked, the spider will simply drop to the ground and hide. The female spends her whole life in her web, while the male leaves the web when he reaches maturity and goes in search of a female.

The male's palp has an elongated femur armed with small knobs and teeth, and there is a pronounced tooth on the tibia, giving him a long reach that helps ensure his safety when he mates. Another protective feature is his carapace, which is armed with teeth along its margins.

SPINY BICEPS SPIDER

Gonatium crassipalpum (Bryant, 1933)

Male

This species is a rich orange-red, and the male's palp has a swollen femur furnished with a number of short, thick spines, giving this spider its common name. I wonder if this arrangement allows the male to get a firmer grip on the female. The vicious hooks on the male's palp (see illustration, right) help to anchor him in position while mating. Secured in this way, the palp is then "inflated" by blood pressure, which in turn "unwinds" the male's sexual organ, causing the embolus to enter the female and the reservoir holding the sperm to be squeezed, injecting sperm into the female's spermathecae.

Size: *Female:* 2.5–3.5 mm
Description: carapace orange with dark eye region; abdomen plain yellow
Microhabitat: low vegetation and at ground level
Distribution: Alberta, Saskatchewan and Manitoba

This spider spins its tiny sheet web among low vegetation, bushes and sometimes at ground level, quite often in forested areas or damp habitats. On a damp morning, you may see numerous webs spread across a grassland or lawn.

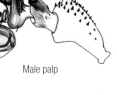
Male palp

151

PINHEAD SPIDER

Walckenaeria directa (O.P. Cambridge, 1874)

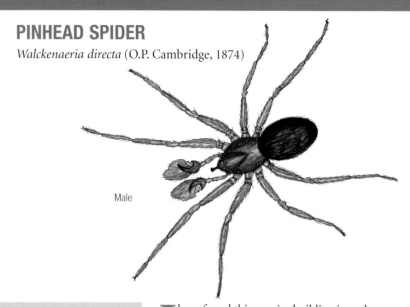

Male

Size: *Female:* 2.5–3 mm

Description: carapace plain brown; abdomen plain dark grey

Microhabitat: ground level

Distribution: British Columbia, Alberta, Saskatchewan and Manitoba

I have found this species building its web across the footprint of a deer in the soft forest floor. Owing to the dampness, the web could be clearly seen.

This particular species illustrates the remarkable head region that many male Linyphids display. The protrusions and knobs are perhaps an adaption to snare the female's fangs so she doesn't harm the male during mating. As the male makes contact with the female, her first reaction is often to sink her fangs into him and inject venom that will paralyze him while she eats him. These head protrusions prevent the fangs from snapping shut. This spider's head "pits" hold the female's fangs harmlessly within their cavities. The various pits in the head region contain hairs that produce a pheromone that we believe calms the female down while the male mates with her.

Male's head

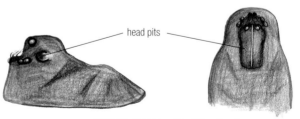

head pits

Head pits of money spider (*W. castanea*)

Heads of Other Linyphiidae Species

Walckenaerianus aimakensis

Walckenaeria dondalei

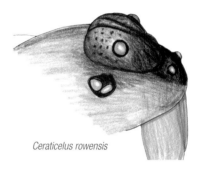

Ceraticelus rowensis

Grammonota gigas

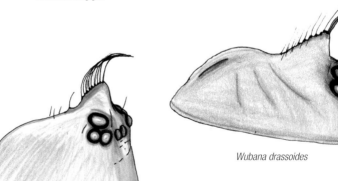

Wubana drassoides

Wubana atypica

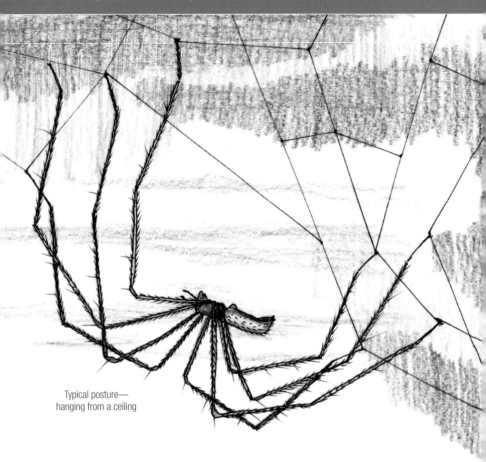

Typical posture—
hanging from a ceiling

Daddy-long-legs Spiders
Pholcidae

Pholcus phalangiodes face

Two genera of Pholcidae have been recorded in Canada, with one species in each. Our region has both species.

This family is one of warm climates, yet because its members make use of houses and buildings, it has become cosmopolitan. These species have been introduced to our area, having arrived among timber, furniture or other items.

These spiders make a scaffold web of loose silk threads that are hard to see unless covered with dust. The spider hangs from the underside of its web, and its long legs enable it to move very rapidly.

Daddy-long-legs have a curious behaviour—the spider vibrates its body when disturbed. The vibrations are so rapid that the spider "disappears" into a blur and cannot be seen. The behaviour is a defence mechanism against predators.

The female is a furious predator that uses her long legs to good advantage in reaching out for prey, which she then bites on just one leg. The venom acts very quickly, preventing any retaliation from the prey.

The egg sac, which the female carries in her jaws, is very flimsy, and the eggs can easily be seen through the few strands of silk that hold them together.

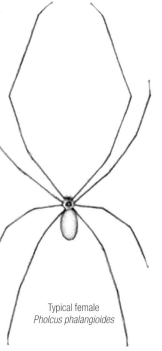

Typical female
Pholcus phalangioides

Female with egg sac

DADDY-LONG-LEGS

Pholcus phalangioides (Fuesllin, 1775)

Male

Unmodified palpal tarsus

Size: *Female:* 8–10 mm

Description: carapace yellow with orange central stripe; abdomen yellow with orange sides

Microhabitat: inside damp buildings

Distribution: British Columbia, Alberta and Saskatchewan; introduced, likely from Europe

These long-legged spiders make tangled webs inside buildings, where they are confined within our region of western Canada. Farther south, they are cosmopolitan, living in subtropical and tropical regions, where they are found outdoors among prickly pear cactus and other vegetation.

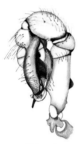

Male palp

This is a true spider and should not be confused with Harvestmen, which are from a different order, Opiliones. Harvestmen have a body in just one part, whereas a spider's body is divided into two segments. A Harvestman has only two eyes, while this spider has eight.

One of the most staggering things about this species is the complexity of the male palpal organ, particularly when you consider that it is an adaptation of the last segment of the palp. Shown above for comparison are the immature/ unmodified papal tarsus and mature male palp.

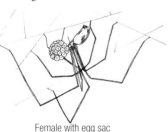

Female with egg sac

The Daddy-long-legs is sure to be found in old buildings where some moisture can be relied on, particularly along the Pacific Coast. It is also found, though uncommonly, in Alberta and Saskatchewan.

ROCK SPIDER
Pholcophora americana (Banks, 1896)

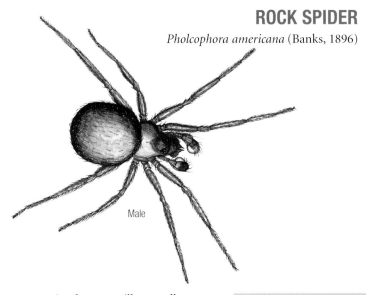

Male

This not a species that you will normally come across—I have included it for interest's sake. This is the second of the two genera within the family Pholcidae. The differences between the genera are striking and can be seen in the size of bodies and the length of the legs, a result of adaptations to their habitats. The Daddy-long-legs (opposite) constructs its snare under an overhang of some sort or in a rigid plant structure such as prickly pear cactus in warmer climates.

Size: *Female:* 1.5–2 mm
Description: carapace light orange; abdomen olive green
Microhabitat: on the ground under slab rocks
Distribution: British Columbia and Alberta

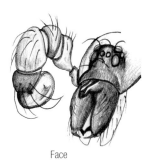

Face

The Rock Spider, as its common name implies, prefers large slabs of rock under which to carry out its life cycle. I have also found it to be quite common deep underground, among the piles of rocks of a mountain rock fall. This habitat can be sampled with the aid of a pitfall trap designed somewhat like a well; a bucket-like pitfall trap is lowered down a pipe to a depth of 2 metres under the ground.

One particular site where this spider can be found is at the famous Frank Slide in Alberta, where part of Turtle Mountain collapsed onto the town of Frank in 1903. This vast expanse of rocks is a wasteland where little grows, yet the Rock Spider flourishes deep among the rubble, likely feeding on tiny insects such as the springtails, proturans and bristletails that abound there.

Spoke-wheel Spiders
Segestriidae

One genus of Segestriidae has been recorded in Canada, containing one species, which is found in our region.

This is a family of six-eyed haplogyne spiders. The first three pairs of legs face forward, an unusual feature in spiders.

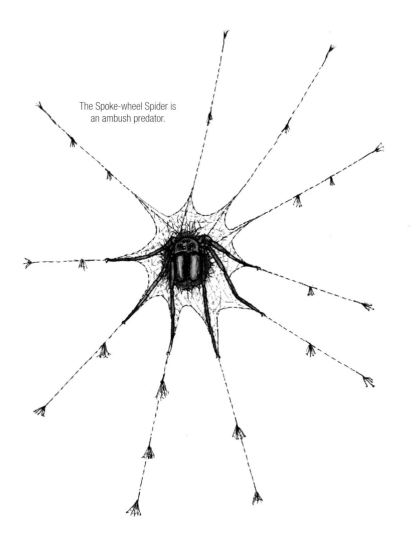

The Spoke-wheel Spider is an ambush predator.

SPOKE-WHEEL SPIDER
Segestria pacifica (Banks, 1804)

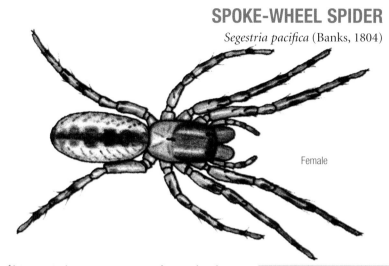

Female

This species' common name refers to the shape of its web. The spider's retreat is usually a hole or crevice in a wall or rock face or under the bark of a tree. A silken tube lines the hole, and radiating out from the entrance of the retreat is a series of trip lines like the spokes of a wheel.

Size: *Female:* 13–22 mm
Description: carapace brown; chelicerae green; abdomen beige with dark cardiac mark
Microhabitat: holes in walls and under tree bark
Distribution: British Columbia

Face

They are beautifully constructed, and each line is raised up on little pylons so as not to snag the substrate. The spider waits just inside the tunnel entrance, with its front legs on the web's skirt. As soon as a prey item touches one of the trip lines, the spider rushes out, stabs the prey through the dorsal abdomen and drags it back into the retreat. This particular method of capture prevents the prey from biting or stinging the spider.

The female lays her eggs inside the retreat and guards the resulting spiderlings until she dies at the approach of winter. The spiderlings eat their mother during the cold season, and then disperse in spring.

Retreat
(adapted from Arthur Smith's drawing in Bristowe's 1958 book, *The World of Spiders*)

159

Long-jawed or Thick-Jawed Orbweavers
Tetragnathidae

Six genera of Tetragnathidae have been recorded in Canada, containing 25 species. Western Canada has 17 species.

"Jaws" of male

Mating embrace of *Tetragnatha montana*—
a way to prevent being eaten

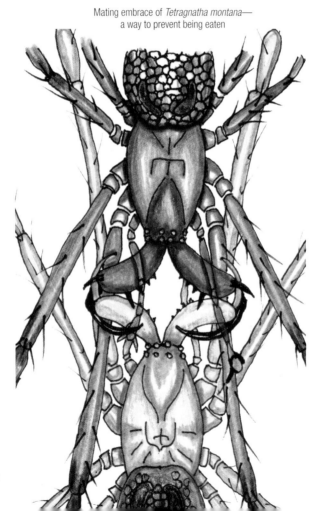

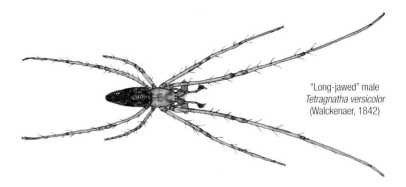

"Long-jawed" male
Tetragnatha versicolor
(Walckenaer, 1842)

Tetragnatha species are elongated spiders with long legs, an elongated abdomen and long jaws. Not only are the chelicerae very long, but the maxillae as well. The name *Tetragnatha* means "four-jawed." Members of the genus *Tetragnatha* are most often found near water.

Pachygnatha xanthosoma

Most genera in this family construct orb webs that are unique in that the web is delicate with very few radii, widely spaced spirals and a small hole in the hub. The hub is bitten out once the frame and spiral threads are in place.

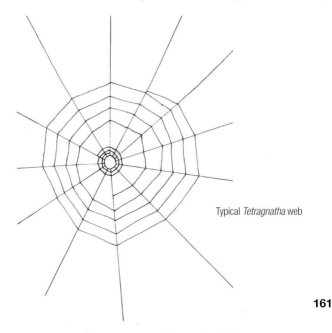

Typical *Tetragnatha* web

161

SILVER LONG-JAWED ORBWEAVER

Tetragnatha laboriosa (Hentz, 1850)

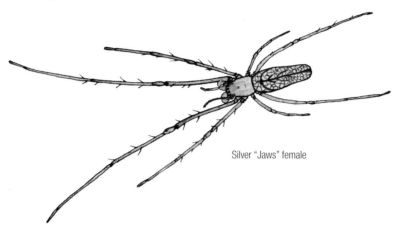

Silver "Jaws" female

Size: *Female:* 6–6.5 mm

Description: carapace orange; abdomen with silver ventral stripes and scraggly, brown lines

Microhabitat: tall meadow grass and shrubs near water

Distribution: British Columbia, Alberta, Saskatchewan and Manitoba

Species in the genus *Tetragnatha* are difficult to identify in the field, so I have chosen to feature *T. laboriosa* owing to its bright silver dorsal colour and the dark band flanked by two silver stripes on the ventral side of the abdomen. *Tetragnatha* species have very long legs and an elongated body and can adopt a pose stretched out along the stems of vegetation in such a way that they almost become invisible. Kathleen and I have laughing named these spiders "Jaws" owing to their very large fangs.

This spider's web has no signal line leading from the hub to a retreat because the spider doesn't build a retreat. Instead, it sits in the middle of the web or rests on nearby vegetation. The web is often covered in small gnats and a few stoneflies.

Ventral side, male

It is my belief that the widely spaced spiral is designed to catch flying insects that have a wide wingspan. I have found the Silver Long-jawed Orbweaver with a near-horizontal web stretched across a small stream.

Male palp

THICK-JAWED HUNTER

Pachygnatha xanthostoma (C.L. Koch, 1845f)

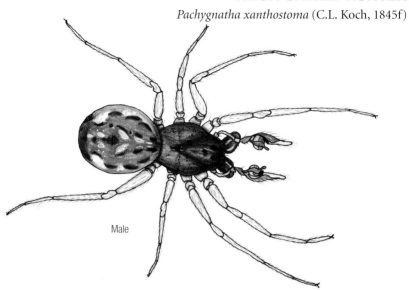

Male

Young spiderlings of this species are found at ground level, where they make small orb webs close to the substrate. However, as a subadult or adult, this spider forsakes its web and turns to actively hunting for its prey, which it does quite high up among the field layer at night. The identification of females is difficult owing to the fact that the epigynum is hidden, as it is in all members of the Tetragnathidae family.

Mating among members of this family is a brutal affair; the male approaches the female head on and seizes her jaws with his enlarged chelicerae (see illustration, p. 160). With the aid of a large tooth on the chelicerae, he wedges her fangs open, then, closing his chelicerae and engaging the hooks, he securely handcuffs her. Now, with his elongated palps, he can reach her sexual opening in safety.

I have found this species in Waterton Lakes National Park in southwestern Alberta and have kept specimens in captivity for observation. Its hunting strategies are much like those of wolf spiders.

Size: *Female:* 3.5–4.5 mm

Description: carapace plain red; abdomen beige with white, edged with black

Microhabitat: on the ground or in the field layer, near water

Distribution: Alberta, Saskatchewan and Manitoba

Male palp

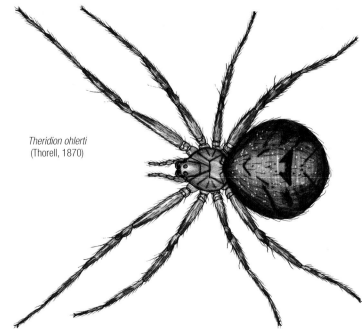

Theridion ohlerti
(Thorell, 1870)

Comb-foot Spiders or Cobweb Weavers

Theridiidae

Fifteen genera of Theridiidae have been recorded in Canada, containing 94 species. Western Canada has 66 species.

This is a family of cobweb weavers, a very general term that could apply to many families of spiders. Members of Theridiidae are unique in that they possess a comb on the tarsus of the hind pair of legs, and for this reason, I prefer the common name "comb-foot spiders." The comb is made up of serrated bristles, which draw viscous silk from the spinnerets and fling it over the spider's prey, ensnaring it and making escape impossible. This is known as a "wrap attack."

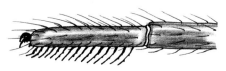

Comb of serrated bristles on tarsus of fourth pair of legs

The web is a three-dimensional, irregular construction of silk. This criss-cross scaffolding web is usually placed close to the ground to snare pedestrian insects, but a few species build aerial snares because they depend on flying insects for food.

Retreat

The female of many comb-foot spider species builds a silken tent in which to house her egg sac. On emerging from the egg sac, the spiderlings remain within the tent until their second moult. Uniquely, the female of some species is capable of feeding her young. The female produces a small droplet of regurgitated fluid from which the young feed. She hangs downward, with the spiderlings jostling each other to get close to her mouth. This mouth feeding continues for several days, after which the spiderlings share their mother's meals. The female will kill and then puncture a prey item in many places to allow the young to eat. The spiderlings form a ball of many bodies and legs around the prey while they feed.

Serrated bristle

Female *Theridion montanum*
(Emerton, 1882)

165

BLACK WIDOW

Latrodectus hesperus (Chamberlin & Ivie, 1935)

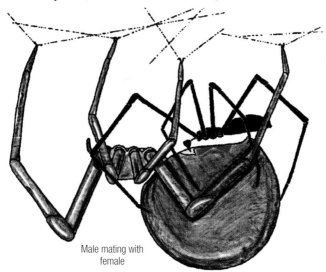

Male mating with female

Size: *Female:* 12–14 mm

Description: carapace black; abdomen shiny black with red hourglass mark on the ventral side

Microhabitat: on the ground under rocks and in campground toilets

Distribution: British Columbia, Alberta and Saskatchewan

Male palp

Black Widows are feared because of their reputedly deadly bite; the large poison glands nearly fill the carapace. Their venom is potent, but it rarely kills a healthy adult human. Any recorded deaths have been of small children or people with health problems. This spider does not "attack," but only bites if it is threatened. Also untrue is the fact that the female always kills the male. This rarely happens, and the female, in fact, is a good mother and even feeds her young.

Poison glands

Spiders in this family have a special comb on their hind legs that "cards" out viscous silk from the spinnerets. This comb enables the spider to launch a "wrap attack" on its prey. By carding out wet, viscid silk, the Black Widow can throw a sticky net over its prey, immobilizing its next meal before any close encounters occur.

166

Male

Black Widows build a scaffold web in which to catch their prey. It is a clever arrangement of silken lines above and below a central horizontal web. The spider hangs beneath the web, where it lives out its life. There are two major purposes to this style of web. One is to snare flying insects, the other is to catch crawling insects.

Look for the red hourglass on the underside of the female's abdomen to identify this species. Only "widows" have this mark.

In the case of a web designed to snare flying insects, the upper tangle of nearly invisible barrage lines cause any insects that crash into them to fall onto the horizontal sheet. This sheet web is studded with drops of glue that help retain the struggling insect. The spider then casts a mass of threads over the prey in a "wrap attack."

The second style of web is designed to snare pedestrian insects. In this case, the scaffolding lines below the central web reach down to the ground and are studded with droplets of glue. The glue snares any insect that bumps into a line. Struggling causes the line, which is elastic and under tension, to lift the insect off the ground, where the victim's struggles are in vain. All the spider has to do now is reel in its meal. One would think that a spider such as the Black Widow, with its potent venom, would simply bite its prey and wait for it to become paralyzed. Not so—the wrap attack comes first, and the paralyzing bite comes later.

Black Widow web

167

FALSE WIDOW
Steatoda borealis (Hentz, 1850)

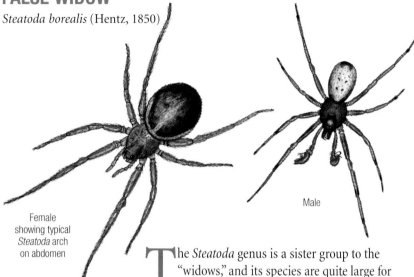

Female
showing typical
Steatoda arch
on abdomen

Male

Size: *Female:* 6.5–10 mm

Description: carapace rich brown; abdomen mauve-brown with anterior cream-coloured crescent

Microhabitat: buildings and woodpiles

Distribution: British Columbia, Alberta, Saskatchewan and Manitoba

The *Steatoda* genus is a sister group to the "widows," and its species are quite large for the Theridiidae family. The False Widow is one of the most common *Steatoda* species and is found across Canada. Many species inhabit human dwellings, and the False Widow is very common in my area of southwestern Alberta. I often find it among our stacks of firewood.

This spider has a rounded abdomen much like a Black Widow but has no hourglass mark on the underside. It can be identified by the cream-coloured crescent on the leading edge of the abdomen.

The male has a well-developed stridulatory apparatus in the form of a series of ridges on the rear of the carapace. He rubs these ridges against opposing teeth under the front edge of his abdomen. The resulting vibrations produce a sound that is used in courtship.

Male palp

Typical web

HOUSE COMB-FOOT SPIDER

Achaearanea tepidariorum (C.L. Koch, 1841)

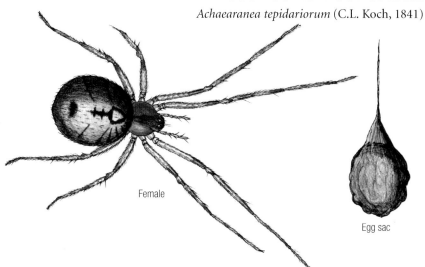

Female

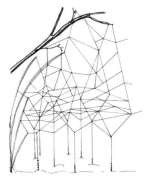

Egg sac

This spider is cosmopolitan in distribution and has been introduced to North America; it is nearly always found in houses or heated greenhouses, particularly in western Canada. A good place to look for it is between the fly screen and a window, for the simple reason that the web shows up in this situation.

The criss-cross scaffolding structure of the web is typical of most comb-foot spiders. The central portion of the web is densely lined with a trellis of threads. Some of the silk is beaded with drops of glue and laid out according to whether the web is designed to catch flying or crawling insects. The web is designed to catch pedestrian insects that bump into the sticky threads attached to the substrate (see illusration, right). The insect's struggles break the threads' sticky contact with the ground, and they pull the insect into midair.

This spider builds a retreat in the upper part of its web. It is an untidy, tent-like structure made of leaves or any other material the female can find. Three or four egg sacs are hung from the web scaffolding.

Size: *Female:* 5–7 mm

Description: carapace beige with dark lines; abdomen beige with darker brown lines and M-shaped mark

Microhabitat: inside buildings

Distribution: British Columbia, Alberta, Saskatchewan and Manitoba; introduced, likely from Central and South America

One type of comb-foot spider web

169

FANGED COMB-FOOT SPIDER

Enoplognatha intrepida (Sorensen, 1898)

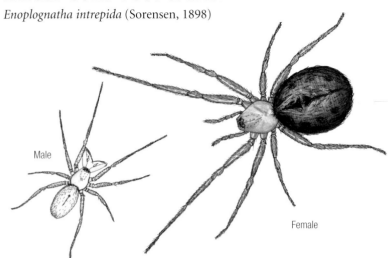

Male

Female

Size: *Female:* 3–5 mm

Description: carapace plain beige; abdomen dark grey with black markings

Microhabitat: on the ground among rocks and on avalanche slopes

Distribution: British Columbia, Alberta, Saskatchewan and Manitoba

Spermathecae, dorsal view

Stridulatory apparatus

This species has been recorded right across Canada, and in western Canada, it is most frequent among rocks above timberline in the Rocky Mountains. I have also found it to be quite common among the rock falls of montane regions.

The "fangs" and chelicerae of the males are greatly elongated and bear a single, large tooth. The female's chelicerae are not elongated and, though she has a single retromarginal tooth, it is not enlarged like the male's. It is presumably a similar adaptation to that of long-jawed spiders, intended to keep the female's poison fangs out of reach while mating.

Fang and tooth

Fanged Comb-foot Spiders have a stridulatory organ on each side of the pedicel, the narrow connection between the carapace and the abdomen. The stridulatory apparatus produces sound, which can sometimes be heard by humans. It consists of a series of fine grooves that are used in conjunction with thorns.

PALE COMB-FOOT SPIDER

Enoplognatha ovata (Clerck, 1757)

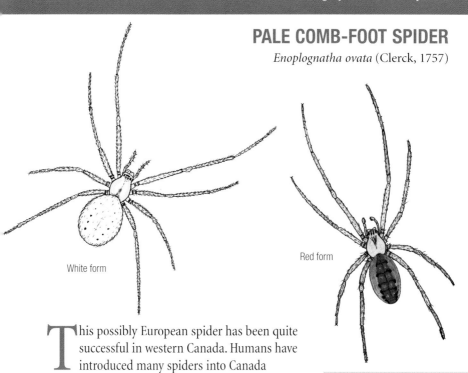

Red form

White form

This possibly European spider has been quite successful in western Canada. Humans have introduced many spiders into Canada without knowing that they have done so, but this species may be native to this country because it is very widespread. This is a point I am unsure of.

The Pale Comb-foot Spider can occur in three colour forms in both sexes, two of which are shown above. The third form has two parallel red bands on the abdomen. Both sexes display a row of paired dots on the abdomen and a pair of dots on either side of the spinnerets.

A good way to find this species is to search for "silked-up" leaves, where the female deposits her very large egg sac, which is a beautiful grayish turquoise colour. If disturbed, she will haul this huge ball of eggs to safety, with some difficulty. The silked-up leaf is a very good retreat because it affords protection, plus there is additional humidity from the leaf's stomata (pores on the underside). The stomata create an exchange of gasses that helps with the spider's respiration.

Size: *Female:* 4–6 mm
Description: carapace yellow with orange central mark; abdomen white or red with black spots
Microhabitat: low vegetation
Distribution: British Columbia and Alberta; introduced, likely from Europe

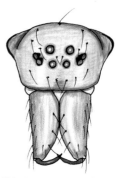

Male showing elongated fangs

171

ANT-EATING COMB-FOOT SPIDER

Euryopis argentea (Emerton, 1882)

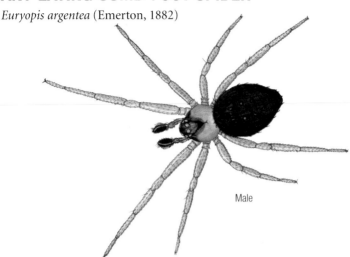

Male

Size: *Female:* 3–4 mm

Description: carapace orange with black head region; abdomen dark brown with conspicuous sigillum

Microhabitat: on the ground among rocks, usually where there are ants

Distribution: Alberta, Saskatchewan and Manitoba

Male palp, ectal view

Male palp

In many families of web-spinning spiders, one or two species forsake spinning a snare and rely on hunting as a means of obtaining their prey; this genus is one of them. I have found this spider hunting among the rocks and stones of a rock fall with a southeastern aspect, making the area quite dry and warm. In this particular spot, there were many small ants and springtails, a possible food source for the spider.

In captivity, I observed a male stalk an ant, which for some reason "froze" in one spot while the spider circled it. The spider laid down threads of silk, which presumably tied its prey to the substrate.

The colour and shape of this spider, along with the six spots on the abdomen (both sexes are similar) make it relatively easy to identify in the field.

The female creates an egg sac of white silk that is anchored to the underside of a rock by bundles or knots of silk.

CUPBOARD SPIDER

Steatoda grossa (C.L. Koch, 1838)

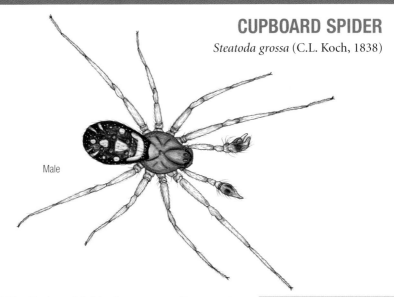

Male

The Cupboard Spider is a cosmopolitan species and is found in many parts of the world, including all three coasts of North America. In western Canada, it is found in our houses or warm outbuildings. It is known as the Brown House Spider in Australia, and it is quite common in Europe.

The effects of the venom of this species are known to be mild in humans, without any long-lasting consequences. Bite symptoms include blistering at the site of the bite and/or a general malaise that lasts for several days. Black Widow antivenom has been shown to be effective for treating Cupboard Spider bites after it was mistakenly administered to a victim who was erroneously believed to have been bitten by the far more dangerous Black Widow.

These spiders are known for preying on Black Widows and Hobo Spiders in areas where the species share a common range.

The male has a stridulatory apparatus that is used to communicate with the female during courtship.

Size: *Female:* 6.5–10 mm
Description: carapace orange; abdomen mauve with cream-coloured spots and blotches
Microhabitat: houses and outbuildings
Distribution: British Columbia

Male palp

Stridulatory apparatus between the carapace and the abdomen

173

CRUSTY-HEAD SPIDER

Crustulina sticta (O.P. Cambridge, 1861)

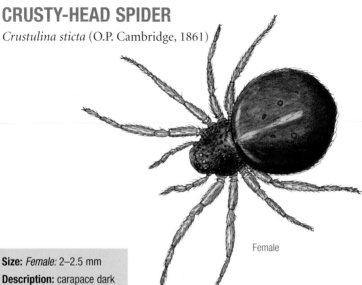

Female

Size: *Female:* 2–2.5 mm

Description: carapace dark brown with many warty granulations; abdomen mauve with yellow T-shaped mark

Microhabitat: in houses, on the ground among grasses or rocks and among cobblestones

Distribution: British Columbia, Alberta and Manitoba

"Crusty" head

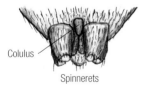

Colulus

Spinnerets

The Crusty-head Spider is a small species of comb-foot spider that occurs in damp habitats such as low vegetation, grass tussocks and detritus. It occurs across our region, with a few gaps in between. I have found it to be sometimes very common while I was collecting with pitfall traps in likely areas.

This species spins a tiny web low down among grass stems. The female with her white egg sac can be found among grass roots when searching by hand. Owing to her small size, use a pooter to collect her.

The tiny, warty granulations on the carapace and sternum can be difficult to make out with a 10x hand lens unless you tilt the specimen to catch the sunlight, which will show the rough texture.

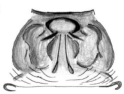

Female epigynum

This species differs from most other Theridiids by having a large colulus, which is a tubercle arising just in front of the spinnerets.

Hackle-band Orbweavers
Uloboridae

Three genera of Uloboridae have been recorded in Canada, containing four species. Western Canada has two species.

Members of the Uloboridae family are found worldwide but are more diverse in the tropics. These spiders are non-venomous; they have no poison glands in their chelicerae (base of the fangs). The very elaborate wrapping of cribellate silk that they spin around their prey is so efficient that poison is not necessary.

Triangular web

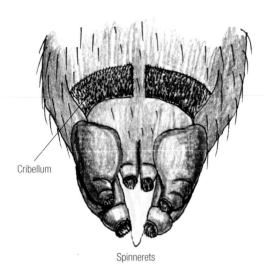

Cribellum

Spinnerets

This family is a group of cribellate spiders that possess an additional spinning organ, the cribellum, which is a small plate located in front of the three pairs of spinnerets. It is densely covered with many hundreds of tiny spigots, each producing a strand of silk. These hackle bands of fine silk are interesting in that they function without any gluey substance. Instead, prey becomes entangled in this silky "wool." The silk is combed out with the aid of a row of specialized bristles that form the calamistrum on the fourth pair of legs. Other families of orb-web weavers produce droplets of glue, which unfortunately deteriorates quickly and is less efficient than the cribellate silk.

Families that contain cribellate spiders include the following:

Blue-silk Spiders (Amaurobiidae);
Mesh-web Spiders (Dictynidae); and
Hackle-band Orbweavers (Uloboridae).

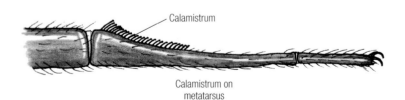

Calamistrum

Calamistrum on
metatarsus

TRIANGULAR-WEB SPIDER

Hyptiotes gertschi (Chamberlin & Ivie, 1935)

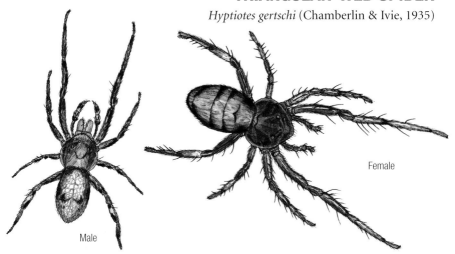

Female

Male

There are two species in this genus in Canada, but only one in our area. I have found this species to be abundant on the east coast of Vancouver Island, enjoying the thick, dense, humid forest there.

Although other members of this family spin orb webs, the Triangular-web Spider only constructs a few segments of a full orb.

If you look carefully at the illustration below, you will notice that the spider is suspended in midair with only its body bridging the gap. It uses its forelegs to hold the web taut, and the slack is held by the third pair of legs. When an insect touches the trap (for this is what the web really is), the spider relaxes the tension on the web, entrapping the prey item. Although this species has no poison glands, it is well able to securely wrap its insect prey in a blanket of cribellate silk before eating it for dinner.

Size: *Female:* 5–6 mm
Description: carapace olive-brown; abdomen beige with light brown sides
Microhabitat: dense, damp forests
Distribution: British Columbia, Alberta, Saskatchewan and Manitoba

Spider with snare

177

FEATHER-LEGGED ORBWEAVER

Uloborus glomosus (Walckenaer, 1841)

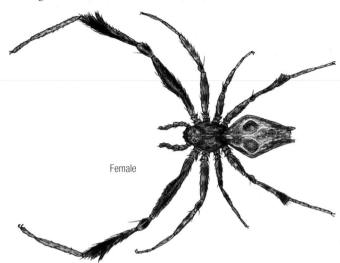

Female

Size: *Female:* 3.5–6 mm

Description: carapace medium brown; abdomen pale mauve with a pair of brown "humps"

Microhabitat: near the ground in grasses and other vegetation

Distribution: Alberta

The Feather-legged Orbweaver builds horizontal webs low down, particularly among grasses. The spider hangs below the web, usually in the hub, in line with a band of silk called a "stabilimentum," which runs right across the web. Spiderlings often create a distinctive spiral stabilimentum in their webs, whereas bigger females sometimes have a long line or even none at all.

The purpose of the stabilimentum is possibly to provide camouflage because it is very hard to see this spider sitting in its web. The feathery sections on the front legs of the female give this spider its common name, and it barely resembles a spider when at rest.

Face

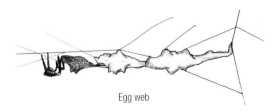

Egg web

Female

Ecribellatae web of *Argiope*,
a genus in the family Aranidae

The strange eye arrangement and the calamistrum on the metatarsus of the fourth pair of legs help identify this species.

The Feather-legged Orbweaver lays down a catching spiral of non-sticky hackle-band silk, which entangles the legs and spines of its prey. In contrast, the orb-web spiders (Araneidae) lay down a catching spiral of a single strand of silk beaded with sticky glue.

The female Feather-legged Orbweaver makes a rudimentary web with just a few radii, a few spirals and a hub. This is where she deposits her egg sacs, which look a lot like wrapped prey insects. She guards the egg sacs for a few days before abandoning them in order to make a fresh web. It is not uncommon for the female to lay several clutches of eggs throughout the summer, as the females of many species do.

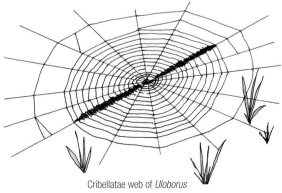

Cribellatae web of *Uloborus*

Glossary

Page numbers indicate where terms are illustrated.

abdomen: the posterior section of a spider's body (below)

ambush predator: a predator that lies in wait for prey to pass by

anterior: situated at the front

anterior median eyes: a pair of eyes at the front of a spider's "face"; eyes often appear shiny

apophysis: a hard projection, located on palpal segments

appendage: a smaller part that is attached to something larger; includes legs, palps and spinnerets (p. 182)

arachnology: the study of spiders (Order Araneae)

araneomorph (*pl.* araneomorphae): a member of the infraorder Araneomorphae, the true spiders

araneophagous: preying on spiders; spider-eating

arboreal: tree-dwelling

autotomy: the voluntary "breaking off" (amputation) of a leg

ballooning: the method by which spiders fly, suspended on the end of a long thread of silk (p. 150)

biennial: having a lifespan of two years

book-lungs: a spider's respiratory organ; true spiders (Araneomorphae) have one pair on the underside of the abdomen, whereas tarantulas and their kin (Mygalomorphae) have two pairs (below)

bridal veil: the silk tie-down threads that a male spider uses to "subdue" a female (p. 109)

bridging line: a thread of silk, played out on the breeze, that once fixed acts as a support for the spider's web

calamistrum: a row of thick hairs used for combing out silk from the cribellum, located on the metatarsus of the fourth pair of legs (p. 126)

carapace: in spiders, the dorsal part of the head (below)

cardiac mark: dark marking or dimple on the dorsal side of the abdomen created by the heart muscle attachments; also called **heart mark**

central hub: the centre of an orb web, a strengthening zone

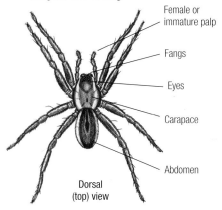

Female or immature palp
Fangs
Eyes
Carapace
Abdomen

Dorsal (top) view

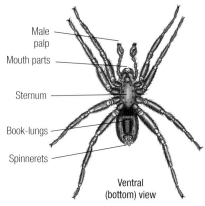

Male palp
Mouth parts
Sternum
Book-lungs
Spinnerets

Ventral (bottom) view

cephalothorax: the head region of a spider, really a fused head and thorax; the legs are attached to the cephalothorax

chelicera (*pl.* chelicerae): basal segments, or jaws, of a spider, ending in apical fangs (below)

claw tufts: dense bunches of hairs between pairs of claws

colulus: a non-functional cribellum, often very small, among the spinnerets (p. 174)

coxa: the first segment of a leg or palp (p. 182)

cribellate: having a cribellum

cribellate silk: feathery, fuzzy silk spun from the cribellum and combed out by the calamistrum; also called **hackled silk**

cribellum (*pl.* cribella): broad, flat plate for spinning silk (p. 42, 126)

detritovore: an organism that feeds on dead or decaying plant or animal matter

dorsal: located on the back; opposite to **ventral**

drag line: silken thread trailed out behind a spider; a safety line

ecribellate: lacking a cribellum

ectal: located near the surface or in an external or outer position

embolus: an organ used by the male to deliver sperm to the female

end feet: the thousands of tiny, flange-like feet at the end of a scopula hair

entelegyne spiders: female spiders that have an external genital opening covered by a hard plate called the **epigyne**

epigyne: a hardened (sclerotized) plate that covers the female genitalia; also called **epigynum**

fang: the apical or end segment of a chelicera, with an opening to a venom gland at its tip (below)

femur: the third segment of a spider's leg (p. 182)

flocculent: a tangle of many strands of silk

folium: a leaf-shaped marking on the dorsal side of the abdomen of some true spiders

formic acid: a defensive fluid that ants spray at a predator

fovea: a small depression in the retina where vision is the most acute

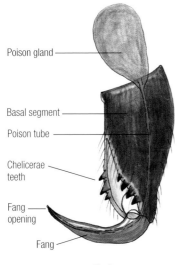

Poison gland

Basal segment

Poison tube

Chelicerae teeth

Fang opening

Fang

Chelicera

Immature or female palp

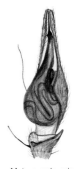

Mature male palp

geographic isolation: the separation of a population of a species from other members of the same species by a physical barrier such as a mountain or body of water; may result in the populations becoming separate species because genetic material cannot be shared

hackled silk: feathery, fuzzy silk spun from the cribellum and combed out by the calamistrum; also called **cribellate silk**

haplogyne spiders: female spiders that have internal genital openings on the epigynum

heart mark: dark mark or dimple on the dorsal side of the abdomen, created by the heart muscle attachments; also called **cardiac mark**

hemolymph: the fluid in the open circulatory system of a spider, bluish in colour; the hydraulics of the legs and other appendages is controlled by hemolymph pressure

Holarctic: a biogeographic region that encompasses most of the Northern Hemisphere, from the North Pole to the Tropic of Cancer

hood: a pocket-like structure at the anterior end of the female's epigynum

inferior claw: an unpaired, or third, claw

knockdown threads: vertical, hanging lines of silk that impede flying insects

laterigrade: laying on its side, against the substrate; usually refers to legs (p. 81)

lock-and-key union: the complex path that the embolus of the male's palp needs to travel to match the path to the female's spermathecae

maxilla (*pl.* maxillae): a spider's mouthparts

mesic: neither very wet nor very dry

metatarsus: the sixth segment of a spider's legs (below)

montane: on or of the mountains

mouth feeding: a method by which some female spiders feed their offspring, i.e., they regurgitate liquid food for their spiderlings

mygalomorph (*pl.* mygalomorphae): a member of the infraorder Mygalomorphae, characterized by having downward-pointing fangs (chelicerae) and two book-lungs; includes tarantulas and folding-door spiders

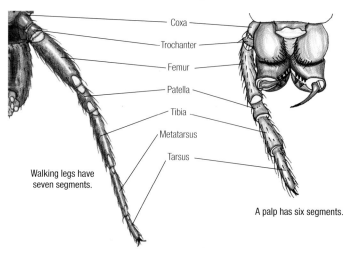

Coxa
Trochanter
Femur
Patella
Tibia
Metatarsus
Tarsus

Walking legs have seven segments.

A palp has six segments.

Nearctic: a biogeographic region that comprises most of North America (to the highlands of northern Mexico) and all of Greenland

palp (*pl.* **palps or palpi**): a male spider's most anterior, leg-like appendages (p. 181)

patella: the fourth segment of a spider's legs and palps; rather short and "knee-like" (p. 182)

pedicel: a narrow, flexible stalk that connects the cephalothorax to the abdomen

pitfall trap: a vessel sunk into the substrate and filled with a preservative into which a spider falls and is trapped

poison gland: the gland containing a spider's venom; housed within the chelicerae (p. 181)

pooter: a series of tubes used to capture and handle small spiders (p. 26)

posterior: located at the back or rear

prostrate: lying flat or along the ground

proturans: tiny, soil-dwelling animals that have no eyes, antennae or wings

pubescence: finely hairy, giving a spider a "mouse-like" appearance

radial threads: the spokes of an orb web

regeneration: the regrowth of a leg inside the coxa

sac retreat: a silken tent used as a retreat (p. 51)

safety line: a drag line of silk

sclerites: a hardened plate, part of the exoskeleton

sclerotized: hardened

scopula (*pl.* **scopulae**): hairs that form a dense pad along the undersurface of the last two leg segments of some spiders (p. 81)

scutum: a hardened (sclerotized) plate on the abdomen of some spiders

secondary eyes: all eyes other than the anterior median eyes; eyes are dark, not shiny

septum: a structure that divides two chambers

sigillum: a reddish-brown spot marking the point of internal muscle attachments

signal line: a tight line of silk running from the hub of a web to the spider's retreat

sperm web: a special, tiny web on which the male deposits a droplet of sperm

spermatheca (*pl.* **spermathecae**): the sperm-storage sac in female spiders

spigots: tiny extensions of the spinnerets from which silk is extruded

spinnerets: silk-spinning organs (below)

spiracle: an opening that allows air into the spider's trachea

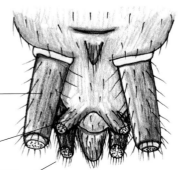

Anterior spinnerets
(attachment disc silk)

Medium spinnerets
(silk for egg sac
or sperm-web)

Posterior spinnerets
(glue, sticky spiral threads)

Six spinnerets

183

stabilimentum (*pl.* stabilimenta): silken bands crossing a web (photo, p. 25)

sternum: a hard, ventral plate (sclerites) on the cephalothorax (p. 180)

stridulatory file: a series of grooves or pegs that produce sound when rubbed together

subalpine: in mountainous areas, the region just below treeline

substrate: surface material

sucking stomach: a reversible "pump" that draws liquids into the spider's digestive system

tapetum lucidum: a reflecting structure in the secondary eyes

tarn: a small mountain lake

tarsus: the seventh and and last segment of the legs and palps (p. 182)

tegulum: a hardened plate (sclerites), part of the male palp

theridiidae comb: a row of bristles on the tarsus of the fourth pair of legs; the bristles are used for "combing out" the silk

tibia: the fifth segment of the legs or palps (p. 182)

touch at a distance: vibrations "felt" by the trichobothrium hairs

tracheal spiracle: an opening to the tracheal system

trichobothrium (*pl.* trichobothria): a long, sensory hair (p. 120)

trip lines: a spider's early warning system of lines of silk that act as "trip wires"

trochanter: the second segment of the legs or palps (p. 182)

true spiders: more "advanced" spiders (not trantulas) having one pair of book-lungs and complex genitalia

tubercle: a small, rounded protuberance

venom: the poisonous substance secreted by spiders and administered by biting

ventral: on the underside, abdominal; opposite to **dorsal**

wrap attack: a type of attack in which a spider wraps its prey in silk before the final "bite"

References

Bristowe, W.S. 1958. *The World of Spiders.* Collins, London, UK.

Dondale, C.D., J.H. Redner, P. Paquin, and H.W. Levi. 2003. *The Orb-Weaving Spiders of Canada and Alaska (Araneae: Uloboridae, Tetragnathidae, Araneidae, Theridiosomatidae).* The Insects and Arachnids of Canada: Part 23. NRC Research Press, Ottawa, ON.

Dondale, C.D., and J.H. Redner. 1990. *The Wolf Spiders, Nurseryweb Spiders, and Lynx Spiders of Canada and Alaska (Araneae: Lycosidae, Pisauridae, and Oxyopidae).* The Insects and Arachnids of Canada, Part 17. Research Branch, Agriculture Canada, Ottawa, ON.

Dondale, C.D., and J.H. Redner. 1982. *The Sac Spiders of Canada and Alaska (Araneae: Clunionidae and Anyphaenidae).* The Insects and Arachnids of Canada: Part 9. Research Branch, Agriculture Canada, Ottawa, ON.

Dondale, C.D., and J.H. Redner. 1978. *The Crab Spiders of Canada and Alaska (Araneae: Philodromidae and Thomisidae).* The Insects and Arachnids of Canada: Part 5. Research Branch, Agriculture Canada, Ottawa, ON.

Foelix, R.F. 1982. *Biology of Spiders.* Harvard University Press, Cambridge, MA.

Hancock, K.M., and J.W. Hancock. 1992. *Tarantulas.* R & A Publishing, Taunton, UK.

Leech, R. 1972. *A Revision of the Nearctic Amaurobiidae (Arachnida: Araneida).* The Entomological Society of Canada, Entomology Research Institute, Canada Department of Agriculture, Ottawa, ON.

Martin, J.E.H. 1977. *Collecting, Preparing, and Preserving Insects, Mites, and Spiders.* Biosystematics Research Institute, Ottawa, ON.

Murphy, F. 1980. *Keeping Spiders, Insects, and Other Land Invertebrates in Captivity.* John Bartholomew and Son, Edinburgh, UK.

Platnick, N.I., and C.D. Dondale. 1992. *The Ground Spiders of Canada and Alaska (Araneae: Gnaphosidae).* The Insects and Arachnids of Canada: Part 19. Research Branch, Agriculture Canada, Ottawa, ON.

Ubick, D., P. Paquin, P.E. Cushing, and V. Roth. 2005. *Spiders of North America: An Identification Manual.* American Arachnological Society.

Websites

American Arachnological Society. www.americanarachnology.org

Tree of Life Web Project, Movies of Jumping Spider Courtship (Wayne Maddison). tolweb.org/accessory/ Movies_of_Jumping_Spider_Courtship?acc_id=64

Tree of Life Web Project, Spiders. tolweb.org/araneae

World Spider Catalog (Version 16.5). www.wsc.nmbe.ch

Index

Entries in **boldface** type refer to the primary species accounts.

spider (cont'd.)
night wolf, 67
northern river
wolf, 68
notch-web, 131
orchard, 134
ornate forest, 64
oviform crab, 114
Pacific buzzing, 46
Pacific sac, 49
pale comb-foot,
171
pinhead, 152
pirate, 91
pirate crab, 113
plain Joe, 62
red-backed
jumping, 96
rock, 157
scorpion crab, 81
six-tailed, 143
snow, 97
spiny biceps, 151
spitting, 105
spoke-wheel, 159
spruce hammock,
148
toad crab, 112
trashline, 26,
136–37
triangle crab, 115
triangular-web,
177
turret, 74
variable running
crab, 87
violin, 107
western Apollo
crab, 84

western funnel-
web, 124
western mesh-
ladder, 140
willow sac, 50
wolf, 24, 78
woodlouse, 53
yellow-legs
jumping, 102
zebra jumping, 94
spitting spider family,
104
spoke-wheel spider
family, 158
stealthy ground
spider family, 54–55
Steatoda
borealis, 168
grossa, 173
stone runner, black,
59
Superphylum
Arthropoda, 17
Synageles
canadensis, 95

T

tarantula, Chilean
rose, 37
tarantulas, 22, 37–38
Tegenaria
agrestis, 122
gigantea, 121
Terralonus
californicus, 92

Tetragnatha
laboriosa, 162
montana, 160
versicolor, 161
Tetragnathidae,
160–61
Thanatus
coloradensis, 83
striatus, 79
Theraphosidae, 22, 37
Theridiidae, 75, 145,
164–65
Theridion
montanum, 165
ohlerti, 164
thick-jawed
orbweaver family,
160–61
Thomisidae, 108–09
Tibellus oblongus, 36,
80, **82**
ticks, 17
tree crab spider
family, 79–80
Trochosa terricola,
65, **67**

U

Uloboridae, 31, 136,
175–76
Uloborus glomosus,
178–79

V

violin spider family,
106

W

Walckenaeria
castanea, 152
direct, **152**
dondalei, 153

Walckenaerianus
aimakensis, 153

wanderer, house, 61

weavers
orb-web, 75
sheet-web, 145

whip-scorpions, 17
tailless, 17

**widow, black,
166– 67,** 168

widow, false, 168

wolf spider family,
65–66

**wolf spider
forest thin-legged,
69
night, 67
northern river, 68**

woodlouse spider
family, 52

Wubana
atypica, 153
drassoides, 153

X

Xysticus
elegans, 116
ellipticus, 114
emertoni, 113
triangulosus, 115

Y

Zelotes fratris, 59

Zygiella nearctica,
131

ABOUT THE AUTHORS

John Hancock

John has been studying spiders for nearly 60 years and became a member of the British Arachnological Society when it was in its infancy. He has a great love for field work and the backcountry.

John studied at the Open University in England while holding down a job driving a London bus. Later, he was fortunate to study under Professor John Cloudsley Thomson at the London University Department of Extra-Mural Studies, completing a diploma in ecology and conservation.

Kathleen and John arrived in Canada in 2000. Their first love was that of true spiders and the outdoors, and they settled in Pincher Creek, Alberta, close to Waterton Lakes National Park. The park's conservation biologist, Kevin Van Tighem, encouraged John to create an inventory of spiders for the park, a project that grew over the years to include the whole of western Canada.

Kathleen Hancock

A lover of all things outdoors, Kathleen was born and grew up in Northern Ireland. She qualified as a teacher and taught in England for 20 years, then started her own business breeding and rearing tarantulas and other arachnids. At the time, little was known about these exotic spiders, and many that were destined for the pet trade died. Kathleen studied there behaviour and natural habitats, passing on her knowledge through her books. She also made captive-bred specimens available to enthusiasts. At one point, she had 4500 live tarantulas at various stages of growth.

Kathleen has taken many of the photographs for this book.